RELIGIOUS REQUIREMENTS AND PRACTICES

of Certain Selected Groups

A HANDBOOK FOR CHAPLAINS

The work involved in developing and producing this
handbook was performed pursuant to contract number
MDA903 76 C 0267 with the
U. S. Department of Defense by:

KIRSCHNER ASSOCIATES, INC.

with subcontract work by:

The Institute for the Study of American Religion

University Press of the Pacific
Honolulu, Hawaii

Religious Requirements andPractices of Certain
Selected Groups:
A Handbook for Chaplains

by
U. S. Department of the Army

ISBN: 0-89875-607-3

Copyright © 2001 by University Press of the Pacific

Reprinted from the 1978 edition

University Press of the Pacific
Honolulu, Hawaii
http://www.universitypressofthepacific.com

PAMPHLET)
)
No. 165-13)

HEADQUARTERS
DEPARTMENT OF THE ARMY
Washington, D.C., 28 April 1978

RELIGIOUS REQUIREMENTS AND PRACTICES

Page

INTRODUCTION

INTRODUCTION

PURPOSE

This Handbook has been prepared for the Office of the Chief of Chaplains, Department of the Army, in order to provide information useful for Chaplains on the beliefs and practices of certain "religious" groups.

Specifically, the purposes of this Handbook are three:

- To facilitate the provision of religious activities which serve the needs of persons of certain faiths not otherwise represented by Military Chaplains and others;

- To define the specific requirements and practices in such a way as to enable Commanders at all levels to make effective personnel decisions in those instances when religious beliefs and practices are claimed to be in conflict with military directives and practices; and

- To provide the specific information about each group in a form which has maximum utility for military purposes, yet is approved as normative or at least acceptable by the leaders of those various groups under study.

The Handbook is written as a guide for Chaplains and, where appropriate, for Commanders. Although it accurately reflects the positions of each group in general, Chaplains are urged to consider the religious needs of each member individual.

The specific purposes of the Handbook also serve to limit the amount of information provided on each group. Thus, while the information provided is accurate (in most instances approved by authorities from the individual groups themselves), it is by no means comprehensive. Lay readers, particularly, are cautioned that the Handbook is not a guide to religion, and that consideration of the implications of adopting a particular faith or belief system is best accomplished under the careful guidance of a Chaplain or other religious leader.

DEVELOPMENT OF THE HANDBOOK

The development of the Handbook was accomplished in a series of steps, the first of which was the selection of the groups themselves. Since there are more than 1,200 religious bodies ("denominations") in the United States, those included in the Handbook were selected on the basis of three specific questions:

- Given the size of the group and the nature of assignments of Army Chaplains, is it likely that members of the group will be found on Army Command posts where no Chaplain of that particular faith or of a related faith is stationed?

- Is the group known to the Office of the Chief of Chaplains as one about which questions have been previously raised by existing Army Chaplains or Commanders?

- Is the nature of the group such that questions about it may be raised by Chaplains or Commanders in the near future?

While the answers to these questions may well encompass many groups not covered in the Handbook, selection of the groups included represents an attempt to incorporate the largest possible percentage of such groups which might be addressed in a single Handbook.

The material presented in the Handbook was derived through an extensive research effort. Pertinent literature was identified and surveyed, various coordinating bodies related to military chaplains were consulted, and open-ended interviews were conducted with active members of the various groups. Based on this research, draft descriptions of each group were developed and prepared for validation.

The process of validating the information included a review of the draft descriptions with officials of the groups. Where possible, approval of the final draft version was obtained from a church or group official (see list of consulting and approving authorities in the Appendix). The final description was then completed, based on the information received from these officials in response to the final draft descriptions.

ORGANIZATION OF THE HANDBOOK

The Handbook includes 37 different group descriptions, divided into seven categories. The categories are:

- Christian Heritage Groups

- Japanese Heritage Groups

- Jewish Groups

- Indian Heritage Groups

- Islamic Groups

- Sikh Groups

- Other Groups

Each section has a brief introductory segment which provides general comments on the category. The 37 different groups are then divided according to the most appropriate category, as they identified it.

The Handbook follows the same format for each group in terms of specific questions raised. In total, 27 different questions were addressed for each organization:

1. HISTORICAL ROOTS:
2. CURRENT WORLD LEADERS:
3. ORIGINS IN THE U.S.:
4. NUMBER OF ADHERENTS IN THE U.S.:
5. ORGANIZATIONAL STRUCTURE:
6. LEADERSHIP AND ROLE OF PRIESTHOOD (MINISTERS, etc.):

7. WHO MAY CONDUCT WORSHIP SERVICES?
8. IS GROUP WORSHIP REQUIRED?
9. WORSHIP REQUIREMENTS:
10. MINIMUM EQUIPMENT FOR WORSHIP:
11. FACILITIES FOR WORSHIP:

12. OTHER SPECIFIC RELIGIOUS REQUIREMENTS OTHER THAN WORSHIP:
13. DIETARY LAWS OR RESTRICTIONS:
14. SPECIAL RELIGIOUS HOLIDAYS:
15. FUNERAL AND BURIAL REQUIREMENTS:
16. AUTOPSY:
17. CREMATION:
18. MEDICAL TREATMENT:

19. UNIFORM APPEARANCE REQUIREMENTS:
20. POSITION ON SERVICE IN THE ARMED FORCES:
21. IS A PRIEST (MINISTER, etc.) REQUIRED AT THE TIME OF DEATH?
22. ANY OTHER PRACTICES OR TEACHINGS WHICH MAY CONFLICT WITH
    MILITARY DIRECTIVES OR PRACTICE:

23. BASIC TEACHINGS OR BELIEFS:
24. CREEDAL STATEMENTS AND/OR AUTHORITATIVE LITERATURE:

    *For some groups, it makes more sense to reverse the
    order of #23 and #24. This is particularly true where
    creeds or authoritative literature form the primary
    core of basic beliefs (see, for example, the description
    on the Church of Christ, Scientist).*

25. ETHICAL PRACTICES:
26. HOW DOES THE *(shortest acceptable name of group)* RECRUIT
    MEMBERS?
27. RELATIONSHIP WITH OTHER RELIGIONS:

Throughout the text, words which are defined in the Glossary of Terms appear

in italics.

Where questions arise about the various groups which are not addressed

in the Handbook, they may be raised directly with the groups themselves, if

necessary, by writing to the individual whose name appears in the upper

right-hand corner of the first page of the group description.

ACKNOWLEDGEMENTS

The Handbook could not have been written without the help of numerous persons who are members of the groups involved, and their work is, of course, gratefully acknowledged.

While it would be impossible to list all who assisted, particular note should be made of the contributions of Dr. Eugene Best of Marist College, Chaplain Simeon Kobrinetz, Mrs. Mary Di Santo, and the Los Angeles Council of Churches, each of whom worked with several different groups.

INTRODUCTION: CHRISTIAN HERITAGE GROUPS

From the arrival of the early pilgrims to the social and political up-
heavals of the 1960s and 1970s, the variety of expressions of the Christian
religion in the United States have been extensive. To chronicle this development would be a monumental task. As of 1977, there are over 800 different,
distinct groups or bodies ("denominations") identified as part of American
Christianity. There have been periods in American history, however, which
have seemed more conducive to the emergence of new Christian bodies than
other periods.

The first variations in American Christianity, of course, were found in
the pre-Revolutionary War colonies. While many of these early settlers were
the forerunners of the larger and better known of the contemporary Catholic and
Protestant churches, others were identified with groups or denominations which
experienced less rapid growth, and, therefore, may be less widely known. Among
these were the Mennonites, principally Dutch, German, and Swiss emigrants, and
the Quakers or "Friends," principally English emigrants. Both of these groups
settled initially in Pennsylvania, and while their history has been strong and
continuous, their growth has been less rapid than other groups.

The 19th century saw the emergence of several new groups, principally as a
result of the religious unrest and revival of the 1830s, and the subsequent
changes in American Christianity which grew out of that period. One of the key
thrusts of this revival period was a renewed interest and belief in the Second
Coming, or Second Advent, of Christ. This focus gave rise to many groups, not
the least of which was the Adventist movement spearheaded by William Miller.
Among the groups established by or emerging from Miller's followers were the
Seventh Day Adventists, the Seventh Day Baptists, and the Church of God. From
the Church of God later came the World Wide Church of God.

The proliferation of Christian groups in the 1830s, together with the concern for the Second Coming, led to the religious quest and subsequent revelation experience proclaimed by Joseph Smith, Jr. Smith established what he termed the "restored" church in 1830. This church, the Church of Jesus Christ of Latter Day Saints, moved west under the leadership of Brigham Young. Some of Smith's followers remained, however, including his son, and around these individuals was established the Reorganized Church of Jesus Christ of Latter Day Saints.

Predictably, the religious actions of the first half of the 19th century led to religious reactions in the last half of that century. Among these reactions, perhaps the strongest was the movement launched by Charles Taze Russell. Russell began to organize his followers in 1872, teaching against what he termed the false teachings of the churches, the tyranny of government, and the oppressions of business. He declared that Jehovah alone was God (that Christ was not divine), and preached against one of the most basic doctrines of the revival period--the depravity of man. Russell announced that the Second Coming had occurred in 1874. Upon Russell's death in 1916, Judge Joseph F. Rutherford became the leader of the movement which later took the name "Jehovah's Witnesses."

Another, though less volatile reaction to the revivalists was in the form of what Sydney E. Ahlstrom has termed the "Harmonial Religions,"[1] concerned with spiritual composure and physical (and even financial) well being. Outgrowths of this movement later were seen in the "new thought" movement (e.g., Dresser) and the "positive thinking" teachings of Peale. The focus on physical health in this period is most prominent in the work of Mary Baker Eddy, founder of the Church

---

[1] Ahlstrom, S., A Religious History of the American People (Garden City, New York: Image Books, 1975); Vol. II, pages f.

of Christ, Scientist. Later manifestations of the new thoughts on Christianity which began during this period include the United Church of Religious Science and the Unity School of Christianity.

While other periods have a great deal of significance in the evolution of the current American Christian scene, the social, education, and political up-heavals of the 1960s seem to have had as great an impact as any other force in any other period. Certainly one of the most widely known and publicized of the 1960s movements was the "Jesus People." Initially finding expression in often radical ways, this movement currently seeks identity with evangelical Christianity in a variety of denominations. Among the current groups growing out of this movement are the Berkeley Christian Coalition (successor to the World Christian Liberation Front), the Children of God (originally "Teens for Christ"), and International Christian Ministeries (formerly Jesus People, International), and The Way.

Perhaps unique in its expression, but indicative of the general climate of interest in the East and the Middle East which now exists, is the Holy Spirit Association for the Unification of World Christianity, also known as the Unification Church, the "Family," and, in less complimentary terms, the "moonies." This movement, initiated by Korean Sun Myung Moon, is one of many "Christian" groups which is not acknowledged as Christian by many of the major Christian bodies in the U.S. Whether or not it is the forerunner of other Christian Missionary movements coming into the U.S. from other countries remains to be seen.

BERKELEY CHRISTIAN COALITION Post Office Box 4309 1825 University Avenue Berkeley, California 94704	Bill Squires AKA: Jesus People, Christian World Liberation Front

HISTORICAL ROOTS: The Berkeley Christian Coalition has its roots in the revival which swept the youth/drug/flower child culture in the late 1960s. The west coast was a major focus of that revival and among the early groups that formed was the Christian World Liberation Front in 1969, which focused its ministry on the great diversity of people living in Berkeley, California. Leadership was provided by Jack Sparks and other former staff people from the Campus Crusade for Christ. In 1975, Sparks and others left to form the New Covenant Apostolic Order. The Christian World Liberation Front was reorganized under the leadership of Bill Squires and reordered as the Berkeley Christian Coalition.

CURRENT WORLD LEADER: Bill Squires.

ORIGINS IN THE U.S.: (See "Historical Roots.")

NUMBER OF ADHERENTS IN THE U.S.: The Coalition is not a church-forming body and hence has no count of adherents. It is located solely in northern California. Its 25 staff members serve Evangelical Christendom of which the coalition is a part.

ORGANIZATIONAL STRUCTURE: The Coalition is organized as a ministry body. Presently, as mentioned above, it has approximately two dozen staff members. A Service Committee coordinates the various ministries and handles administrative concerns. This committee is the activity hub of the Berkeley Christian Coalition because it both serves as the coordinating unit for all other ministries and handles the administrative and financial concerns for each, i.e., typing, mailings, disbursement of monies, maintenance of property, etc.

BERKELEY CHRISTIAN COALITION	Page 2

Organization, Leadership, Worship

ORGANIZATIONAL STRUCTURE (continued): A six-member Council governs the Coali-

    tion, with meetings held on a weekly basis. Council members are repre-

    sentatives of the Service Committee and of each of the following six Coali-

    tion ministries: (1) Abrigo Ranch, which provides a rural setting where

    new Christians can live and work together and obtain spiritual nourish-

    ment; (2) campus ministry, an outreach to nearby students at U.C.

    Berkeley; (3) the Crucible, providing long and short courses emphasizing

    the implications of the Lordship of Jesus Christ for all of life; (4)

    Dwight House, a drop-in center providing temporary housing, counseling

    and referral services to people and travelers in Berkeley; (5) the

    Spiritual Counterfeits Project, responsible for understanding, exposing,

    and effectively countering those broad patterns of spiritual deception

    within our culture, and analyzing the specific cults perpetrating that

    deception; (6) RADIX, a bi-monthly periodical with a current circulation

    of approximately 12,000 in the San Francisco Bay area and around the

    country.

LEADERSHIP AND ROLE OF LEADERS: Leadership is exercised by the Service Com-

    mittee and the Council of ministry representatives. In addition, staff

    persons also function as leaders. They give guidance, foster study of

    the Bible and Christianity, care for people in need, conduct research of

    other religions and spread the gospel to believers and non-believers as

    well.

WHO MAY CONDUCT SERVICES? Not applicable.

IS GROUP WORSHIP REQUIRED? Yes (see "Worship Requirements").

BERKELEY CHRISTIAN COALITION	Page 3
Worship, Requirements, Position on Service	

WORSHIP REQUIREMENTS: Each member is required to be a member of a church.

MINIMUM EQUIPMENT FOR WORSHIP: Not applicable.

FACILITIES FOR WORSHIP: None.

OTHER SPECIFIC RELIGIOUS REQUIREMENTS OTHER THAN WORSHIP: Each member must
make a statement of faith (see "Basic Teachings or Beliefs").

DIETARY LAWS OR RESTRICTIONS. None.

SPECIAL RELIGIOUS HOLIDAYS: None, except those of the individual churches
attended by members of the Coalition.

FUNERAL AND BURIAL REQUIREMENTS: None.

AUTOPSY: No restrictions.

CREMATION: No restrictions.

MEDICAL TREATMENT: No restrictions.

UNIFORM APPEARANCE REQUIREMENTS: No restrictions.

POSITION ON SERVICE IN THE ARMED FORCES: The goals of the coalition include
opposition to violence, but no official position has been taken (see
"Ethical Practices").

IS A PRIEST OR CLERGYPERSON REQUIRED AT TIME OF DEATH? No.

ANY OTHER PRACTICES OR TEACHINGS WHICH MAY CONFLICT WITH MILITARY DIRECTIVES
OR PRACTICES: None.

BASIC TEACHINGS OR BELIEFS: Teachings and beliefs of the Coalition are summarized in the six statements in their Statement of Faith, as follows:
(1) We believe that the Scriptures are the uniquely inspired Word of God
and are fully authoritative in matters of faith and practice; (2) We believe that there is one God, eternally existent in three persons; the

BERKELEY CHRISTIAN COALITION	Page 4

Basic Beliefs, Literature, Ethics

BASIC TEACHINGS OR BELIEFS (continued): Father, the Son and the Holy Spirit, who are of one substance and equal in power and glory; (3) We believe in the historic virgin birth of Jesus the Messiah who was both fully God and fully human, that He lived a sinless life and that He died on the Cross as a sinner's substitute of sin; that He rose again from the dead and ascended to the right hand of God to perform the ministry of intercession; and that He shall come again, personally and visibly, to complete the eternal plan; (4) We believe that Man and Woman were created in the image of God but through disobedience fell from a sinless state; that from the Fall, the entire race of humanity was sentenced to eternal death; and that from this condition men and women can be delivered by the grace of God through faith, on the basis of the Work of Christ; (5) We believe in the ministry of the Holy Spirit, the third person of the Godhead, who applies the work of Christ to men and women through justification, re-generation, and sanctification, and that He makes it possible for a person who believes in Christ to live a godly life in this present world which is under Satan's dominion; (6) We believe in the spiritual unity of all true believers in Christ; that these believers who are committed to Jesus Christ as Lord, are thus recognized as His Church.

CREEDAL STATEMENTS AND/OR AUTHORITATIVE LITERATURE: (See also "Basic Teach-ings and Beliefs.") The Coalition accepts the Bible as the only author-ity for faith and life.

ETHICAL PRACTICES: Summarized in the five Coalition goals, the practices are as follows: (1) We are committed to making disciples of our King; (2)

BERKELEY CHRISTIAN COALITION	Page 5

Ethics, Recruiting, Relationships

ETHICAL PRACTICES (continued): Integral to discipleship is the search for a truly Christian lifestyle which includes a life of ecological and economic simplicity, practical sharing, love and care for one another, and rejection of the use of physical and psychological manipulation and violence; (3) Discipleship also requires the development of a distinctly Christian world view which includes a prophetic critique of the world and a positively stated alternative to the death-dealing systems of this world; (4) We each seek to produce beauty and encourage creativity; (5) We desire to substantially restore dignity and humanness to life.

HOW DOES THE BERKELEY CHRISTIAN COALITION RECRUIT MEMBERS? The Coalition sponsors internship work/study programs whereby interested persons can become involved in the various ministries of the Coalition while studying or working in the community. This internship program aids those who are served by the various ministries and it also assists the interns in learning more about the Coalition's purpose and activities. Interns can decide whether to join the staff in order to deepen their involvement. In addition, the Coalition has an active evangelistic program which includes personal witnessing, literature distribution, public programs and rallies, and involvement in social service.

RELATIONSHIP WITH OTHER RELIGIONS: The Coalition is one with Christians of all denominations. It does, however, take a strong stance against groups that operate from an occult and/or eastern religious base. Through its Spiritual Counterfeits Project it publishes literature and cassette

I-10

BERKELEY CHRISTIAN COALITION	Page 6

Relationships

RELATIONSHIP WITH OTHER RELIGIONS (continued): tapes to expose and counter these groups. It has also involved itself in confrontation with these groups at public rallies, meetings, debates, and in court.

THE CHILDREN OF GOD Box 11021 Chicago, Illinois 60611	Matt Child Correspondence Office For the United States

HISTORICAL ROOTS: The Children of God evolved out of revivalist movements affecting the California youth culture in the late 1960's led by the Rev. David Brandt Berg. At first they took the name "Teens for Christ" and later were called the Children of God by the news media, after Berg's followers travelled through the United States on an Exodus-like trek in 1969, settling in Texas in 1970. Although the focus of much controversy, the Children became a highly mobile and evangelical body and continued to grow. In the mid-seventies they have attempted to replace their revolutionary image with one more conservative, emphasizing a settled existence of colonies in urban centers.

CURRENT WORLD LEADER: There is no world leader. Each colony is independent and self-governing, united only in their goals of "loving the lost and evangelizing the world." Moses David, a name chosen by Rev. Berg, writes letters of fatherly counsel and advice to all colonies and the general public.

ORIGINS IN THE U.S.: (See "Historical Roots.")

NUMBER OF ADHERENTS IN THE U.S.: There are approximately 500 American Members in 60 colonies in major U.S. population centers. They claim to have countless additional friends and supporters who work for Jesus but do not reside in the communes. Many more Americans are included in the 7,500 members involved in overseas missions in 72 countries.

ORGANIZATIONAL STRUCTURE: Each colony is headed by a shepherd who is elected by the colony members. Each three colonies are grouped together into a district with a district shepherd elected by the colony shepherds and

THE CHILDREN OF GOD   Page 2

Organization, Leadership

ORGANIZATIONAL STRUCTURE (continued): approved by the next level up (the

    regional shepherd), or appointed by the colony shepherds. This pattern

    is followed with districts being grouped together into regions, etc.

    Each local colony is autonomous and the overseeing shepherds offer

    suggestions, teach classes, and help to coordinate witnessing efforts

    in their area. According to the need, some countries or language areas

    will have an information and correspondence center that serves the

    general public. The only international operation of the group is the

    gathering of news and events worldwide and published bi-monthly and

    sent to all members and subscribers in a magazine called, The New

    National News. Moses David's position is that of a father figure

    writing letters of fatherly council and advice to his children around

    the world.

LEADERSHIP AND THE ROLE OF MINISTERS: Each colony is governed by its local

    council (comprised of all members of the colony with three months

    membership or more) which is headed by the shepherd. All decisions are

    by majority vote of the council members. Although the colonies are a

    voluntary association, they generally aspire to follow the guidelines

    of the writings of Moses David. Converts desiring to serve full time

    in Gospel ministry undergo leadership training and are then ordained

    for the Gospel ministry. Colony shepherds or elders are formally or

    informally chosen by the members. Often these shepherds will be a

    married couple.

Worship, Requirements

WHO MAY CONDUCT WORSHIP SERVICES? Within a colony, usually the shepherd

or someone the shepherd appoints, conducts inspirational meetings. Out-

side the colonies (i.e., someone who is not able to live full time in a

colony, such as a person in the armed services), anyone may call a ser-

vice.

IS GROUP WORSHIP REQUIRED? No, but all are encouraged to attend evening

gatherings for prayer and Bible study, and to worship as individuals.

WORSHIP REQUIREMENTS: A convert or "babe Christian" first spends much time

studying the Bible, the teachings of Moses David, and participating in

group prayers.

MINIMUM EQUIPMENT FOR WORSHIP: Daily reading of the Bible and MO Letters

(See "Literature"). Communion with bread and wine may be practiced.

FACILITIES FOR WORSHIP: Any place suitable where Children of God gather.

OTHER SPECIFIC RELIGIOUS REQUIREMENTS OTHER THAN WORSHIP: Colony members

are required to "forsake all" and follow Jesus in order to be able to

go into all the world and preach the gospel. Members living away from

a colony report monthly on witnessing activity and correspond regularly

with the nearest colony. Individual members can volunteer their ser-

vices for other colonies where needed, and generally aspire to be

overseas missionaries.

DIETARY LAWS FOR RESTRICTIONS: None, but members are encouraged to eat

"healthful" foods.

SPECIAL RELIGIOUS HOLIDAYS: Christmas, Easter, and Thanksgiving.

FUNERAL AND BURIAL REQUIREMENTS: None.

THE CHILDREN OF GOD	Page 4

Requirements, Basic Beliefs

AUTOPSY: Permitted.

CREMATION: Permitted.

MEDICAL TREATMENT: No restrictions, although initial cures may be attempted
by praying over sick member.

UNIFORM APPEARANCE REQUIREMENTS: Neat and orderly.

POSITION ON SERVICE IN ARMED FORCES: The Children of God have tended to
avoid military service, claiming ministerial exemption for members.

IS A CLERGYPERSON REQUIRED AT TIME OF DEATH? No.

ANY OTHER PRACTICES OR TEACHINGS WHICH MAY CONFLICT WITHIN MILITARY DIREC-
TIVES OR PRACTICES: The Children of God requests CO status for
members. Many members who have served in the armed forces have requested non-combatant status.

BASIC TEACHINGS AND BELIEFS: The Children of God base their teachings on
the Bible, the Revolutionary handbook of Jesus Christ, as expounded by
their prophetic leader, Moses David. They believe that all people have
sinned, and that the wages of sin is death, but that the gift of God
is eternal life. They believe that all evil governments will suffer
God's judgments and that the motivation of much of established society
is corrupt; i.e., greed and selfishness. They believe that much of
the religious establishment is doing little to teach their members to
evangelize the world, but that there are millions of other Christians
who really witness and win souls both in and out of the churches.
They believe that God has in His love sent His Son Jesus Christ into
the world so that all who believe in Him will be saved by faith

THE CHILDREN OF GOD	Page 5

Basic Beliefs, Literature, Ethics, Recruiting

BASIC BELIEFS (continued): (Eph 2:8&9). Following the New Testament example, they sell all that they have, give all property and income to the Children of God, and hold all things in common. They believe that they are given power by the Holy Spirit to witness for Jesus, and that this Holy Spirit sends them into the world to preach the Gospel to others. They believe that disciples must be willing to avoid worldly entanglements, and to suffer affliction gladly.

CREEDAL STATEMENTS AND/OR AUTHORITATIVE LITERATURE: The Children of God accept as equal in authority the Bible and those of Moses David's writings which are inspirational and prophetic. Both are considered to be the word of God. The writings of Moses David are published in a series of letters, called MO Letters.

ETHICAL PRACTICES: Ethical guidelines are drawn from the Bible as interpreted by Moses David. Children of God are expected to be quiet and orderly, to obey the law and officers of the law, to show respect for owners of property and officials of schools and establishments. Children of God are not allowed to use narcotics and tobacco. They believe in marriage with permanent mates with divorce being a very rare exception. Sex is seen as a normal and healthy function of marriage. Children of God are encouraged to fill their life with witnessing and Bible study.

HOW DO THE CHILDREN OF GOD RECRUIT MEMBERS? They engage in active witnessing by word of mouth and by distributing literature, greeting people and talking with them, handing out copies of the MO Letters. Prospective young members, especially those alienated from the mainstream society,

THE CHILDREN OF GOD	Page 6

Relationships

HOW DO CHILDREN OF GOD RECRUIT MEMBERS (continued): are promised the experience of a loving, supportive community. The colonies attempt to fulfill
   this promise.

RELATIONSHIP WITH OTHER RELIGIONS: Children of God are eager to share their
   faith with others. The overzealousness of a new early members was
   viewed as offensive to some churches they contacted, but this was never
   their policy. Many times they have found acceptance and cooperation
   among various sectors of the Church and World Council of Churches, and
   have developed open and cooperative relationships on mutual goals of
   world evangelism.

THE CHURCH OF CHRIST, SCIENTIST Christian Science Center Boston, Massachusetts 02115	J. Buroughs Stokes, Manager Committees on Publication AKA: Christian Science

HISTORICAL ROOTS: Founded in Boston in 1879 as "a church designed to commemorate the word and works of our Master (Christ Jesus), which should rein-
state primitive Christianity and its lost element of healing." The
Church's founder, Mary Baker Eddy, had a Protestant Christian background,
having grown up as a devout Congregationalist.

CURRENT WORLD LEADER: Mr. James Spencer, President of the Mother Church for
1977-78. A new President is appointed annually (in June) by the Christian
Science Board of Directors.

ORIGINS IN THE U.S.: A lifelong Bible student, Mrs. Eddy was healed of a severe injury in 1866 as she read the account of one of Jesus' healings in
the New Testament. The healing led her to the conviction that healing
through prayer is a natural and normal aspect of the Christian experience
and to the discovery of what she understood as the Science of Christianity
She later wrote the Christian Science textbook (1875), established the
Church of Christ, Scientist (1879), and established the Christian Science
periodicals, including The Christian Science Monitor (1908).

NUMBER OF ADHERENTS: The Church has approximately 3,000 branches in more than
50 countries. However, because of a permanent requirement in the Church
Manual, specific statistics on membership are not released.

ORGANIZATIONAL STRUCTURE: The Church of Christ, Scientist, consists of the
Mother Church, the First Church of Christ, Scientist, in Boston, and
branches throughout the world. Governing bylaws are published in the
Church Manual written by Mrs. Eddy. Manual provisions are administered

| THE CHURCH OF CHRIST, SCIENTIST | Page 2 |

Organization, Leadership, Worship

ORGANIZATIONAL STRUCTURE (continued): by a Board of Directors, who appoint
chief officers of the Mother Church. Branch churches are democratically
self-governed. They choose officers from their congregation by election
for limited periods of office.

LEADERSHIP AND THE ROLE OF THE PRACTITIONERS: The church has no clergy.
Christian Science practitioners are lay members who devote full time to
the public Christian healing ministry of Christian Science. Practitioners
hold no special church offices unless elected to them, like any other
member of the congregation.

On-base ministry to service personnel and dependents is provided
through Christian Science field workers accredited by the Mother Church,
and include Chaplains, Christian Science Ministers for Armed Services Personnel, and Christian Science Representatives in the Armed Forces. As
appropriate, field workers hold Sunday and mid-week worship services, conduct Sunday School for those under 20, supply Christian Science literature
to those desiring it, and provide Christian Science treatment through
prayer when called upon. They also assist students of Christian Science
in the military to participate in local branch church activities.

WHO MAY CONDUCT WORSHIP SERVICES? Formal services are conducted by two lay
Readers, elected by members of each branch church or society from their
own congregation. Readers usually serve for 3 years. While the church
has no ordained clergy, chaplains are provided in the military.

THE CHURCH OF CHRIST, SCIENTIST	Page 3

Worship, Requirements

IS GROUP WORSHIP REQUIRED? No. (See also "Facilities for Worship.") Christian Scientists consider attendance at services a privilege, and ordinarily attend whenever it is possible for them to do so.

WORSHIP REQUIREMENTS: No ritual or liturgical religious practices or requirements. Members ordinarily study daily the weekly Bible "lesson-sermons" read at Sunday church services. Mrs. Eddy instructed members to pray daily: "'Thy kingdom come;' let the reign of divine Truth, Life, and Love be established in me, and rule out of me all sin; and may Thy Word enrich the affections of all mankind, and govern them!"

MINIMUM EQUIPMENT FOR WORSHIP: None. Services center around selections of readings from the Bible and the denominational textbook, Science and Health with Key to the Scriptures by Mary Baker Eddy.

FACILITIES FOR WORSHIP: Recognized branch churches and Christian Science Societies meet in their own buildings if possible, or in rented space. Informal groups of Christian Scientists may meet for worship in the spirit of Jesus' words in Matthew: "For where two or three are gathered together in my name, there am I in the midst of them."

OTHER SPECIFIC RELIGIOUS REQUIREMENTS OTHER THAN WORSHIP: Dedicated members may apply for Primary Class Instruction from an authorized Teacher of Christian Science. This instruction lasts two weeks; in addition, a one-day meeting is held in each subsequent year.

    The Mother Church holds an Annual Meeting on the Monday following the first Sunday in June. Although not required, dedicated members normally try to attend whenever feasible.

THE CHURCH OF CHRIST, SCIENTIST   Page 4

Requirements, Position on Service

OTHER RELIGIOUS REQUIREMENTS (continued): Christian Science conferences for

    Military Personnel and Workshops for field workers are held periodically

    in designated areas under the auspices of the Mother Church.

DIETARY LAWS OR RESTRICTIONS: Members abstain from the use of alcohol, to-

    bacco, and drugs.

SPECIAL RELIGIOUS HOLIDAYS: None.

FUNERAL AND BURIAL REQUIREMENTS: Matters of individual decision.

CREMATION: Many members elect it, but it is a matter of individual choice.

AUTOPSY: Not a practice, except under special circumstances.

MEDICAL TREATMENT: A Christian Scientist relies on spiritual means alone

    through prayer for healing. Normally members would request exemption

    from medical care and treatment, as well as a permanent waiver of immu-

    nizations on the ground that it is inconsistent with religious convic-

    tions ("legitimate religious objection" - AR40-562).

UNIFORM FOR APPEARANCE REQUIREMENTS: None.

POSITION ON SERVICE IN THE ARMED FORCES: Individual decision. Members have

    served in the military in wartime and peace time, while others seek

    alternative service.

IS A PRACTITIONER OR OTHER REQUIRED AT TIME OF DEATH? No.

OTHER PRACTICES OR TEACHINGS WHICH MAY CONFLICT WITH MILITARY DIRECTIVES OR

    PRACTICE: None.

CREEDAL STATEMENTS AND/OR AUTHORITATIVE LITERATURE: The teachings of Chris-

    tian Science are rooted in the Bible. The basic theological and ethical

THE CHURCH OF CHRIST, SCIENTIST   Page 5

Literature, Basic Beliefs, Ethics

CREEDAL STATEMENTS AND/OR AUTHORITATIVE LITERATURE (continued): statement of

Christian Science is the denominational textbook, Science and Health with

Key to the Scriptures by Mary Baker Eddy.

BASIC TEACHINGS AND BELIEFS: The brief religious tenets of Christian Science

are given on p. 497 of Science and Health, and read: "1. As adherents

of Truth, we take the inspired Word of the Bible as our sufficient guide

to eternal life. 2. We acknowledge and adore one supreme and infinite

God. We acknowledge His Son, One Christ; the Holy Ghost or divine Com-

forter; and man in God's image and likeness. 3. We acknowledge God's

forgiveness of sin in the destruction of sin and the spiritual under-

standing that casts out evil as unreal. But the belief in sin is pun-

ished so long as the belief lasts. 4. We acknowledge Jesus' atonement

as the evidence of divine, *efficacious* Love, unfolding man's unity with

God through Christ Jesus the Way-Shower; and we acknowledge that man is

saved through Christ, through Truth, Life, and Love as demonstrated by

the Galilean Prophet in healing the sick and overcoming sin and death.

5. We acknowledge that the crucifixion of Jesus and his resurrection

served to uplift faith to understand eternal Life, even the allness of

Soul, and the nothingness of matter. 6. And we solemly promise to watch

and pray for that Mind to be in us which was also in Christ Jesus; to do

unto others as we would have them do unto us; and to be merciful, just

and pure."

ETHICAL PRACTICES: The moral code of Christian Science is contained in the

Ten Commandments and the Sermon on the Mount (see also "Literature").

THE CHURCH OF CHRIST, SCIENTIST   Page 6

Recruiting, Relationships

HOW DOES THE GROUP RECRUIT MEMBERS? Historically, the Church's main thrust

of outreach has been its ministry of Christian healing. This is reflec-

ted both in the work of practitioners and members, and in the Church

periodicals, The Christian Science Journal, Christian Science Sentinal,

and The Herald of Christian Science. The Christian Science Monitor, an

international newspaper, reflects the Church's basic redemptive purpose

in the context of specific social concern.

RELATIONSHIP WITH OTHER RELIGIONS: The Church participates in interfaith or

ecumenical activities on local, national, and international levels.

Representatives have served as consulting or associate members in local

councils of churches, have attended as invited guests or delegates to

various interfaith conferences, and have taken part in denominational-

level ecumenical dialogue.

Participation in interfaith activities is limited by the fact that

the Church does not prescribe political or social positions for members

nor engage as a denomination in joint social programs. Emphasis is on

the healing ministry and on the spiritual education of individuals to

their social responsibility as Christians.

CHURCH OF JESUS CHRIST OF LATTER DAYS SAINTS 50 East North Temple Salt Lake City, Utah 84150	Spencer W. Kimball President AKA: The Mormons; LDS

HISTORICAL ROOTS: Organized during period of unrest and "revival" in the U.S.

during the 1800s. Joseph Smith, Jr., confused as to which of the various

Protestant denominations was the True Church, prayed for divine insight.

In answer to this prayer, God the Father and Jesus Christ appeared to him

to inform him that none were right, but that the fulness of the gospel

would be revealed to him in the future. Later, the Angel Moroni delivered

to him an ancient record, on metal plates, containing the history and

religious teachings of a people who had migrated from Jerusalem to America

some 600 years before Christ. These people, believed by the Mormons to be

forefathers of at least some of the American Indians, had recorded their

religious experiences, including a record of their encounter with the

resurrected Christ. These were translated and published by Joseph Smith,

Jr., and are known as "The Book of Mormon."

CURRENT WORLD LEADER: Spencer W. Kimball, President.

ORIGINS IN THE U.S.: (See also "Historical Roots.") Organized on April 6,

1830, in the home of Peter Whitmer in Fayette, NY, by Joseph Smith, Jr.,

and five others. Joseph Smith, Jr. was the first President of the Church.

From New York, the Mormons moved to the midwest. Expelled from Illinois,

they were led by Brigham Young, the second President of the Church, to the

basin of the Great Salt Lake.

NUMBER OF ADHERENTS IN THE U.S.: As of December, 1976, 2,366,572 persons in

the United States were among the 3,742,749 members worldwide.

ORGANIZATIONAL STRUCTURE: The Mormons are organized with a three-member First

Presidency, the Council of Twelve Apostles, and the First Quorum of

ORGANIZATION (continued): Seventy which administers the *ecclesiastical*

    affairs of the Church. There is also a Presiding Bishopric, which admin-

    isters the temporal affairs of the Church under the direction of the

    First Presidency, and a Patriarch. These members are referred to as the

    General Authorities. Membership is organized into Stakes and Wards, or

    into Missions, Districts, and Branches. A stake consists of 6 to 10 wards

    with a Stake President and two counselors, assisted by a High Council of

    12 members and other stake leaders with advisory responsibility over

    specific programs of the wards. A ward is a congregation of 300 to 800

    members within a limited geographical area, functioning under the direc-

    tion of a Bishop and two counselors, assisted by department or auxiliary

    heads who supervise the Sunday School, Women's Auxiliary, Young Men's and

    Young Women's programs, etc. Military Chaplains are lay members whose

    special training and experience qualify them for service.

LEADERSHIP AND ROLE OF PRIESTS: LDS have a lay leadership. Qualified and

    worthy members are called to positions of leadership to serve without com-

    pensation. General Authorities (see "Organizational Structure"), called

    on a full time basis, devote the remainder of their lives to these call-

    ings. Others serve in addition to their normal occupations for a limited

    time, often 5 to 7 years. All worthy males are ordained to the priest-

    hood either Melchizedek (High Priesthood) or Aaronic (lower Priesthood).

WHO MAY CONDUCT WORSHIP SERVICES? General Authorities, Stake and Mission Pres-

    idents, Bishops and Branch Presidents, LDS Chaplains and servicemen Group

    Leaders may conduct services.

CHURCH OF JESUS CHRIST OF LATTER DAY SAINTS	Page 3
Worship, Requirements	

IS GROUP WORSHIP REQUIRED? It is expected of all members, and required for full fellowship and privileges.

MINIMUM EQUIPMENT FOR WORSHIP: Sufficient bread and water in trays and cups to administer the Sacrament (Communion).

FACILITIES FOR WORSHIP: Usually conducted in worship chapels; services may be held in any place affording atmosphere for quiet and reverence.

OTHER SPECIFIC RELIGIOUS REQUIREMENTS OTHER THAN WORSHIP: Members are expected to adhere to the Gospel of Jesus Christ, must be baptized by proper authority, live a Christian life, and observe the counsel of the Church leaders. Members are expected to contribute *tithing* to the Church.

DIETARY LAWS OR RESTRICTIONS: Tea, coffee, tobacco, and strong drink (including all alcoholic beverages) prohibited; moderation in all things is admonished. Meat, fruits and vegetables should be eaten in proper proportions conducive to good health.

SPECIAL RELIGIOUS HOLIDAYS: None.

FUNERAL AND BURIAL REQUIREMENTS: LDS chaplains may assist the local and/or home ward bishop. Where LDS Chaplain is not available, the nearest local bishop or branch president should be notified, as well as the family of the deceased. When necessary, an LDS Chaplain may conduct conduct funeral and/or graveside services. If burial occurs in combat area where no bishop or LDS Chaplain is available, a worthy member holding the Melchizedek Priesthood may conduct a simple service or memorial. LDS Chaplains may conduct services for nonmembers if requested.

CHURCH OF JESUS CHRIST OF LATTER DAY SAINTS	Page 4
Requirements, Position on Service, Basic Beliefs	

AUTOPOSY: No restrictions.

CREMATION: Not encouraged, but left to family. If cremated, regular funeral services may be held.

MEDICAL TREATMENT: No restrictions for seriously ill, injured or wounded. Life sustaining treatment depends on laws and individual conscience.

UNIFORM APPEARANCE REQUIREMENTS: Generally none. However, members who have made covenants with the Lord in a Church Temple are privileged to wear "temple garments" underneath military or civilian clothing.

POSITION ON SERVICE IN THE ARMED FORCES: The Mormons believe in responding to the call of their government to serve in the armed forces, particularly in defense of the country. However, the decision to serve in time of voluntary service is a personal matter for each individual member.

IS A MINISTER REQUIRED AT TIME OF DEATH? No. If desired, worthy Melchizedek Priesthood members may administer a blessing to the sick and dying.

ANY OTHER PRACTICES OR TEACHINGS WHICH MAY CONFLICT WITH MILITARY DIRECTIVES OR PRACTICES: Closed Communion (Sacrament) is required. No robes or other special paraphernalia used in worship. LDS Chaplains should not participate in any activities which conflict with accepted practices and policies of the Church.

BASIC TEACHINGS OR BELIEFS: LDS "Articles of Faith" state: "(1) We believe in God the Eternal Father, and in His Son, Jesus Christ, and in the Holy Ghost. (2) We believe that men will be punished for their own sins, and not for Adam's trangression. (3) We believe that through the Atonement of Christ, all mankind may be saved, by obedience to the laws and

CHURCH OF JESUS CHRIST OF LATTER DAY SAINTS   Page 5

Beliefs

BASIC BELIEFS (continued): ordinances of the Gospel. (4) We believe that the

first principles and ordinances of the Gospel are: first, Faith in the

Lord Jesus Christ; second, Repentance; third, Baptism by immersion for

the remission of sin; fourth, Laying on of hands for the gift of the Holy

Ghost. (5) We believe that a man must be called of God, by prophecy, and

by the laying on of hands, by those who are in authority to preach the

gospel, and administer in the ordinances thereof. (6) We believe in the

same organization that existed in the Primitive Church, namely, apostles,

prophets, pastors, teachers, evangelists, etc. (7) We believe in the

gift of tongues, prophecy, revelation, visions, healing, interpretation

of tongues, etc. (8) We believe the Bible to be the word of God as far

as it is translated correctly; we also believe the Book of Mormon to be

the word of God. (9) We believe all that God has revealed, all that He

does now reveal, and we believe that He will yet reveal many great and

important things pertaining to the Kingdom of God. (10) We believe in

the literal gathering of Israel and in the restoration of the Ten Tribes;

that *Zion* (the New Jerusalem) will be built upon the American continent;

that Christ will reign personally upon the earth; and, that the earth

will be renewed and receive its paradisaical glory. (11) We claim the

privilege of worshiping Almighty God according to the dictates of our

own conscience, and allow all men the same privilege, let them worship

how, where, or what they may. (12) We believe in being subject to kings,

presidents, rulers, and magistrates, in obeying, honoring, and sustaining

the law. (13) We believe in being honest, true, chaste, benevolent,

CHURCH OF JESUS CHRIST OF LATTER DAY SAINTS — Page 6

Basic Beliefs, Literature, Ethics, Recruiting, Relationships

BASIC BELIEFS (continued): virtuous, and in doing good to all men; indeed, we may say that we follow the admonition of Paul - We believe all things, we hope all things, we have endured many things, and hope to be able to endure all things. If there is any thing virtuous, lovely or of good report or praiseworthy, we seek after these things."

CREEDAL STATEMENTS AND/OR AUTHORITATIVE LITERATURE: The King James version of the Bible, the Book of Mormon, and the revelations given to other Presidents of the Church ("Doctrine and Covenants" and "The Pearl of Great Price") are accepted as scripture.

ETHICAL PRACTICES: (See also "Dietary Laws or Restrictions" and "Basic Beliefs," especially articles 12 and 13.) Teachings of the Church prohibit sex outside of marriage, do not accept homosexuality or abortions (except where necessary to preserve the life of the mother), and teach "doing good to all men."

HOW DOES LDS RECRUIT MEMBERS? The Church actively *proselytizes* through its Missionary program. Persons wishing membership are interviewed by Church authorities for worthiness and commitment to the teachings of the Church. Upon approval, they receive baptism, later followed by the laying on of hands for receiving the gift of the Holy Ghost.

RELATIONSHIP WITH OTHER RELIGIONS: (See "Basic Beliefs," articles 11.)

| GENERAL CONFERENCE OF SEVENTH-DAY ADVENTISTS
6840 Eastern Avenue, N.W.
Washington, D.C. 20012 | Elder Clark Smith
Director
National Service Org. |

HISTORICAL ROOTS: Traced to the Millerite movement of the 1830s and 1840s in the United States. William Miller (1782-1849), a Baptist from Vermont, developed a deep concern about the Second Coming (Second Advent) of Christ through years of Biblical study. Preaching and lecturing throughout the northeastern United States, Miller drew followers from all of the Christian churches, all drawn by this message that, indeed, the "kingdom of God is at hand." Following his death in 1849, a small but strong group of believers remained, including those who were to be drawn together into what became the Seventh-Day Adventist church.

CURRENT WORLD LEADER: Robert H. Pierson, President of the General Conference of Seventh-Day Adventists.

ORIGINS IN THE U.S.: Following 1844, a date established by Millerites as the date prophesied in Daniel for the Second Advent, those adherents of the Millerite movement who had come to accept the observance of the Seventh-day Sabbath were drawn together. In 1860, the Seventh-Day Adventists incorporated the publishing house in Michigan, publishing the inspired writings of Mrs. Ellen G. White, and beginning the organization of churches and groups of churches into conferences. The General Conference was organized in Battle Creek, Michigan in 1868, then moved to the Washington, D.C. area in 1903.

NUMBER OF ADHERENTS IN THE U.S.: Approximately 500,000.

ORGANIZATIONAL STRUCTURE: Local churches are constituent members of conferences, which are constituent members of union conferences, which are constituent members of the General Conference of Seventh-day Adventists.

GENERAL CONFERENCE OF SEVENTH-DAY ADVENTISTS   Page 2

Organization, Leadership, Worship

ORGANIZATIONAL STRUCTURE (continued): Military liaison is arranged through
    the National Service Organization of the church with representatives on
    all levels above the local church.

LEADERSHIP AND THE ROLE OF MINISTERS: Ordained ministers may perform all
    ecclesiastical duties. *Ordination* is dependent upon the recommendation
    of a conference committee (see "Organizational Structure") and confir-
    mation by the union conference, usually following four years of field
    work in the churches after graduation from a three-year seminary pro-
    gram. During the four years of service in the field, seminary graduates
    are termed "licensed ministers" and may perform *ecclesiastical* duties
    only in the local church to which they are assigned. Ministers (both
    licensed and ordained) are given their credentials and are under the
    direction of the conference organizations. Spiritual leadership is the
    work of pastors on the local church level, conference, union confer-
    ence, and General Conference officers and departmental directors.

WHO MAY CONDUCT WORSHIP SERVICES? Any member.

IS GROUP WORSHIP REQUIRED? No.

WORSHIP REQUIREMENTS: No specific requirements.

MINIMUM EQUIPMENT FOR WORSHIP: Bible and Hymnbook.

FACILITIES FOR WORSHIP: Any moderately quiet area with suitable privacy.

ANY OTHER SPECIFIC RELIGIOUS REQUIREMENTS OTHER THAN WORSHIP: None. How-
    ever, "worship" is regarded as including adherence to the Ten Command-
    ments.

GENERAL CONFERENCE OF SEVENTH-DAY ADVENTISTS	Page 3

Requirements, Position on Service

DIETARY LAWS OR RESTRICTIONS: An ovo-lacto (egg-milk) vegetarian diet is suggested as ideal for health, but "clean" meats (from animals which have a split hoof and chew the cud, as per Leviticus 11) may be added to the diet by individual decision (e.g., beef, lamb). No alcoholic beverages or smoking are accepted.

SPECIAL RELIGIOUS HOLIDAYS: Weekly Sabbath is celebrated from sundown Friday to sundown Saturday (see also "Position on Service in the Armed Forces").

FUNERAL AND BURIAL REQUIREMENTS: Individual preferences are honored.

AUTOPSY: No restrictions.

CREMATION: Individual preferences are honored.

MEDICAL TREATMENT: No restrictions.

UNIFORM OR APPEARANCE REQUIREMENTS: No restrictions.

POSITION ON SERVICE IN THE ARMED FORCES: Noncombatancy is strongly taught, but individual belief is honored. Observance of the Seventh-day Sabbath (see "Special Religious Holidays") is a requirement for membership. Normally during Sabbath hours only those duties which pertain to the saving or preserving of human life or alleviation of suffering are engaged.

IS A MINISTER REQUIRED AT TIME OF DEATH? No.

OTHER PRACTICES OR TEACHINGS WHICH MAY CONFLICT WITH MILITARY DIRECTIVES OR PRACTICES: (See also "Position on Service in the Armed Forces.") Seventh-Day Adventists regard the nation or state as the outgrowth of God's instruction that people or communities should band together to prevent evil men from harassing individuals in the community with

I-32

GENERAL CONFERENCE OF SEVENTH-DAY ADVENTISTS   Page 4

Basic Beliefs, Literature, Ethics, Recruiting

OTHER PRACTICES OR TEACHINGS WHICH MAY CONFLICT WITH MILITARY DIRECTIVES OR
    PRACTICES (continued): resultant chaos. The individual is to "submit"
    to the government and give it his/her support and allegiance in all
    items that would not result in beliefs or actions that would cause dis-
    obedience to God.

BASIC TEACHINGS OR BELIEFS: Seventh-Day Adventists believe that all are
    sinners in need of salvation. Salvation is attained only through grace
    ("unmerited favor") extended freely by God if accepted by the individual.
    Observance of the Ten Commandments (including the Sabbath of the Fourth
    Commandment) is directed for all who accept the forgiveness of their
    sins and salvation from God, not for the purpose of gaining salvation,
    but because of appreciation for salvation extended and in observance of
    Christ's words, "If ye love me, keep my commandments."

CREEDAL STATEMENTS AND/OR AUTHORITATIVE LITERATURE: Seventh-Day Adventists
    have no creed as such. The Old and New Testaments of the Bible, ex-
    cluding the Apocrypha, are considered authoritative. The writings of
    Mrs. Ellen G. White are regarded as inspired by God, though the Bible
    is regarded as supreme and by it her writings are evaluated.

ETHICAL PRACTICES: Determined by the individual member in the light of Bible
    instruction and, to a lesser extent, the writings of Mrs. E.G. White.

HOW DOES THE ADVENTIST CHURCH RECRUIT MEMBERS? By encouraging Bible study
    and encouraging those who thoroughly understand the teachings and
    practices of the Seventh-Day Adventist Church to receive baptism by
    immersion and membership in the church.

GENERAL CONFERENCE OF SEVENTH-DAY ADVENTISTS	Page 5

Relationships

RELATIONSHIP TO OTHER RELIGIONS: In view of their belief in salvation

   through the grace of God and belief in the Bible as God's Word of truth,

   Seventh-Day Adventists are normally included in the group of Evangelical

   Protestant churches. Their efforts for relief in the form of food,

   clothing, and shelter for the victims of disasters, either separately

   or in cooperation with other churches and groups, are well known.

HOLY ORDER OF MANS	Rt. Rev. Andrew Rossi
20 Steiner Street	Steward, Esoteric
San Francisco, California 94117	Council

HISTORICAL ROOTS: The Holy Order of MANS (Mysterion, Agape, Nous, Sophia) was founded in 1968 in the United States. It was the result of some 30 years of preliminary work of, and revelation to, Father Paul Blighton, late Director General of the Order. The idea of the order evolved, under Father Paul's guidance, from the findings of a group of professional people interested in the welfare of humanity both now and in the future. Born out of revelation, the Order has its roots in the living presence of Jesus Christ as the living Word for this present Age. The Order also uses the ancient wisdom teachings, and in particular the writings of Paul the Apostle, who in the first century of Christianity worked to unify all churches.

CURRENT WORLD LEADERS: Leadership is vested in Mother of the Order, Ruth Blighton, and in the Office of the Director General. Present Steward of the Esoteric Council is the Rt. Rev. Andrew Rossi (see "Organizational Structure").

ORIGINS IN THE U.S.: (See "Historical Roots.")

NUMBER OF ADHERENTS IN THE U.S.: There are approximately 600 people under life vows, 200 in training, and over 1,000 attached to Christian Communities as lay adherents. Many are enrolled in the Discipleship program, a correspondence program.

ORGANIZATIONAL STRUCTURE: Authority in the Order is vested in the Director General's Office, now under the care of a Steward and the Esoteric Council. The Council includes 10 regional directors. Order centers are called Brotherhouses. Each Brotherhouse is headed by a Rev. Father. The

HOLY ORDER OF MANS   Page 2

Leadership, Worship

ORGANIZATION (continued): Order has 60 centers in the U.S., plus one each

in Canada, Japan, Germany, France, Holland, England, and Spain.

LEADERSHIP AND ROLE OF PRIESTS AND MINISTERS: (See also "Organizational

Structure.") The Holy Order of MANS is a disciplined order. Members who

wish to affiliate as a full member go through a rigorous program of train-

ing. Applicants must first be approved by the Esoteric Council to begin a

novitiate training. After 3 months under a vow of obedience, the trainee

appears before a regional council for an interview and takes temporary

vows. The candidate now begins a year of training in philosophy, Bible

studies, and self development. Each candidate works full time and donates

earned income.

Following this year, the candidate moves to the missionary training

program and serves a year in either the Brown Brothers of the Holy Light

(males) or the Immaculate Heart Sisters of Mary (females). During this

year a vow of celibacy is added to the temporary vows. The year is

oriented on selfless service. At the end of the year, life vows are

administered--vows of service, humility, obedience, poverty and purity.

Following the taking of vows, 2 years of on-the-job training in Order-

related programs are required.

Upon application to the Esoteric Council, the members of the Order

may be admitted to advanced training for ministry. This advanced train-

ing completed, they may become either priests or ministers.

WHO MAY CONDUCT WORSHIP SERVICES? Priests conduct most, but ministers may

conduct some services.

Worship, Requirements

IS GROUP WORSHIP REQUIRED? No, but it is encouraged.

WORSHIP REQUIREMENTS: Communion services are held each morning, and daily
     prayer services are held each evening.

MINIMUM WORSHIP EQUIPMENT: *Chalice, paten,* 3 law candles, olive oil, and a
     seven and five branch candlestick.

FACILITIES FOR WORSHIP: Worship services normally are held in chapels which
     are included in each center.

OTHER SPECIFIC RELIGIOUS REQUIREMENTS OTHER THAN WORSHIP: Members of the Order
     are required to fast one day a week (see also "Leadership and Role of
     Priests and Ministers").

ANY DIETARY LAWS OR RESTRICTIONS: None, except narcotics are prohibited.

SPECIAL RELIGIOUS HOLIDAYS: Christmas, Easter, The Ascension, Pentecost, and
     the founding day of the Order (July 24).

FUNERAL AND BURIAL REQUIREMENTS: The body is to remain at rest for 3 days
     before disturbing it. Embalming is prohibited; cremation preferred.

AUTOPSY: Not allowed.

CREMATION: Preferred and recommended.

MEDICAL TREATMENT: Members refrain from use of drugs for any purpose as far
     as possible. Chiropractors are preferred. The Order believes in and
     practices spiritual healing. Traditional medical services are used
     whenever necessary.

UNIFORM APPEARANCE REQUIREMENTS: Members wear clerical clothes from the
     earliest stages of their training.

Position on Service, Beliefs

IS A PRIEST OR MINISTER REQUIRED AT TIME OF DEATH? Not required, but prefer-
    red.

ANY OTHER PRACTICES OR TEACHINGS WHICH MAY CONFLICT WITH MILITARY DIRECTIVES
    OR PRACTICE: Although the teaching of the Order promotes harmlessness and
    nonviolence, the Order does not actively oppose military service, per se.

BASIC TEACHINGS OR BELIEFS: The Order teaches the Universal Law of Creation,
    in accordance with the teachings of Jesus, accepted as Master of the Order
    and in accordance with the transcendent unity of all being in God. The
    Order has no creed as such, but operates out of a base of mystical, con-
    templative Christianity. Mystical experience is encouraged through
    prayer, meditation, and spiritual exercises. Teachings are generally sum-
    med up in the "prayer of the Brothers," expressed in poetic form as fol-
    lows: "I strive, O Father, Creator of all, To be a Nameless Wanderer, To
    be perfect and all sufficient, So poised, so balanced, That none but SELF
    can comprehend. All of this was unknown, unknowable. The greatness, the
    splendor, the magnificance of All, with the Majesty of Thy Powers, I, more
    than mind of man can conceive. For in the Beginning, O Father, all know-
    ing, Thou didst speak the Word, And the Word was with Thee, and the Word
    was Thee. And the greatness and the splendor Of Thy Power didst manifest
    Not through Mind, but Thy Self. For then the Word took flesh, and The
    Great Being of the Christos was born in all Magnificence and Power. For
    this is the mystery that man has not understood. For Thy Word Thou spok-
    est once again, God in great humility, Sealed in the fleshly body of the
    little child, Thus was the Master Jesus born. My every prayer shall be,

Beliefs, Literature, Ethics, Recruiting, Relationships

BASIC BELIEFS (continued): and is, That in this Holy Family I be received,
    To be the servant of all, To receive the great call. Glory, glory, glory,
    Lord God of All. Amen."

ADDITIONAL NOTES ON BASIC BELIEFS: The purpose of the Order is Service to the
    Creator through service to all fellowman. Members may work within the
    Order or at an outside job. The Order strives to help the seeking one
    attain the true Light of Christ.

CREEDAL STATEMENTS AND/OR AUTHORITATIVE LITERATURE: (See also "Basic Teach-
    ings or Beliefs.") The New Testament is considered authoritative. The
    Order also publishes numerous books and materials which are used in its
    study programs and teaching work. Of prime importance are 3 volumes:
    Book of The Master Jesus, Golden Force, and Golden Nuggets.

ETHICAL PRACTICES: Each member of the Order leads an extremely disciplined
    life of service to humanity. Each takes a lifetime vow of poverty, ser-
    vice, humility, purity, and obedience.

HOW DOES THE HOLY ORDER OF MANS RECRUIT MEMBERS? The Order does not *prosely-
    tize*. Members are attracted to the Order by hearing of its work and
    service, or through its Christian community and discipleship programs.
    Some members are Street Missionaries who are available on the streets for
    counseling, direction, or other help.

RELATIONSHIP WITH OTHER RELIGIONS: The Order is considered to be non-
    sectarian and non-demoninational. They seek the unifying principles in
    all religions, teaching the laws of creation as revealed by Christ Jesus,
    and found also at the core of all true spiritual teaching. Those seeking

HOLY ORDER OF MANS   Page 6

Relationships

RELATIONSHIP WITH OTHER RELIGIONS (continued): entrance into the Order may

   retain membership in any church with which they may have previously been

   associated.

HOLY SPIRIT ASSOCIATION FOR THE UNIFICATION
  OF WORLD CHRISTIANITY
4 West 43rd Street
New York, New York 10036

Susan Reinbold
Director of Public Affairs

AKA: The Unification Church

HISTORICAL ROOTS: On Easter morning in 1936, while 16-year-old Sun Myung Moon

was in deep prayer on a mountainside in Korea, Jesus Christ appeared to

him to tell him he had an important mission to accomplish in the fulfill-

ment of God providence. For the next nine years, Sun Myung Moon studied

intensely and struggled to prepare himself for his responsibility. In

those years of prayer, he discovered a series of principles which made it

possible to understand the spiritual and physical nature of the universe,

the patterns and meaning of history, as well as the inner meanings of the

parables and symbols of the Bible and the purpose of all religions.

Rev. Moon began his public ministry in what is now North Korea and

was imprisoned by the Communists for preaching the Word of God. After

being liberated from the three-year imprisonment, Rev. Moon moved his

work to Seoul, Korea, where in 1954 he formally established the Church.

CURRENT WORLD LEADER: Although the Unification Church has missions in over

120 countries, there is no formal international structure. Each country

operates autonomously. Rev. Sun Myung Moon is considered the Prophet

and, therefore, spiritual leader of the Church.

ORIGINS IN THE UNITED STATES: The Unification Church was brought to the

United States in 1959, by Dr. Young Oon Kim, who settled in Eugene, Ore-

gon, and translated the Divine Principle, revealed to Rev. Moon, into

English. In 1972, the Unification Church of America was given a spur to

growth when Rev. Moon began several national speaking tours. Rev. Moon

travels extensively throughout America, and resides in Tarrytown, New

York with his wife and 9 children.

HOLY SPIRIT ASSOCIATION FOR THE UNIFICATION | Page 2
OF WORLD CHRISTIANITY

Organization, Leadership, Worship

NUMBER OF ADHERENTS IN THE U.S.: 30,000

ORGANIZATIONAL STRUCTURE: The Unification Church is focused in its national

offices in New York City, and is headed by its national President,

Mr. Neil A. Salonen. Local Resident Centers function in all 50 States

and Puerto Rico; each is headed by a director appointed by the national

office. Besides the local centers, the Unification Church encounters

the public through a number of subsidiary structures which seek to

implement specific parts of the Church program: International Family

Association (IFA), Collegiate Association for the Research of Principles

(CARP), High School Association for the Research of Principles (HARP), and

the Performing Arts Department which has a variety of groups, e.g., New

Hope Singers International, Korean Folk Ballet, Sunburst (folk-rock

group), Voices of Freedom (gospel group), and Go-World Brass Band.

In 1975, Rev. Moon founded the Unification Theological Seminary in

Tarrytown, New York. The Seminary offers a 2-year Master of Religious

Education (M.R.E.) program designed to develop students' abilities in

theology, Biblical studies, religious education and philosophy.

LEADERSHIP AND ROLE OF MINISTERS: The Unification Church does not emphasize

the ordained ministry. Local congregations are organized as a family

model with a director or church elder (male or female) organizing the

Center's activity.

WHO MAY CONDUCT SERVICES? Each core member is, on a rotational basis,

encouraged to give the sermon or conduct the service.

HOLY SPIRIT ASSOCIATION FOR THE UNIFICATION   Page 3
   OF WORLD CHRISTIANITY

Worship, Requirements, Position on Service

IS GROUP WORSHIP REQUIRED: No, but if a person lived with a local center,

   he would be expected to meet with other members at least once a day.

WORSHIP REQUIREMENTS: Public worship services are held twice weekly, on

   Sunday and Wednesday evening. Members can go to either or both.

MINIMUM WORSHIP EQUIPMENT: None

FACILITIES FOR WORSHIP: Any simple meeting room.

OTHER SPECIFIC RELIGIOUS REQUIREMENTS OTHER THAN WORSHIP: Celibacy until

   marriage.

DIETARY LAWS OR RESTRICTIONS: No official laws; alcohol or tobacco are

   generally not used.

SPECIAL RELIGIOUS HOLIDAYS: The Unification Church recognizes the traditional

   Christian holidays, and has four holidays of its own. Because some of

   these are determined by the lunar calendar, the exact day of the year

   will vary: God's Day (January 1); Parent's Day (April); Day of All

   Things--World Day (June); Children's Day (November).

FUNERAL AND BURIAL REQUIREMENTS: To be conducted by a Church elder.

AUTOPSY: No restrictions.

CREMATIONS: No restrictions.

MEDICAL TREATMENT: No restrictions

UNIFORM APPEARANCE REQUIREMENTS: No restrictions.

POSITION ON SERVICE IN THE ARMED FORCES: The Unification Church emphasizes the

   responsibility of citizenship but sets no official rules as to military

   service.

HOLY SPIRIT ASSOCIATION FOR THE UNIFICATION   Page 4
   OF WORLD CHRISTIANITY

Position on Service, Basic Beliefs

IS A MINISTER OR CLERGY PERSON REQUIRED AT TIME OF DEATH?   A Church member is
   desirable.

ANY OTHER PRACTICES OR TEACHINGS WHICH MAY CONFLICT WITH MILITARY DIRECTIVES
   OR PRACTICE: None

BASIC TEACHINGS OR BELIEFS: The teaching of the Unification Church, the
   Divine Principle, can largely be divided into three parts.   The most
   fundamental part of the Principle is the "Principle of Creation" which
   explains who God is and how and why He created.

   The Church teaches that the Infinite God can be known by the study
of His Creation.   Everything exists in pairs - masculine and feminine,
positive and negative, initiative and receptive.   God contains the same
polarity.   All things also contain an inner and outer nature.   In like
measure, God's Internal Nature (Sung-sang) is His heart of infinite love,
and His External Form (Hyung-sang) is the energy of the universe.

   God created the universe to bring Himself joy and to bring joy to
man.   Every man and woman has the capacity to fully reflect the image of
God and become one with Him.   We achieve that oneness when we come to
develop fully our capacity to love.   In family life, we ideally find the
most complete expression of the range and depth of human love.

   God's love is the infinite counterpart of the three modes of human
love - love of parents for children, love of husband and wife, and love of
children for parents.

   Since God is the substantial being of goodness and the eternal ideal,
in accordance with His purpose, man was also created to become the ideal

BASIC BELIEFS (continued): embodiment of goodness, in whom sin and suffering

would be a contradiction and an impossibility. The reality of the con-

tradictions and evil in which man finds himself is a result of his having

lost his original value by falling. Traditional Christianity calls this

state of man "the fall" and its details, motivation and process are found

in the section of the Principle entitled "The Fall of Man."

The men fallen into sin must tread the path of salvation under God's

blessing; in the Unification Principle, salvation is restoration. In

other words, the purpose of salvation is to return to the original state

before the fall; therefore, God's providence of salvation is the provi-

dence of restoration. The section "Principle of Restoration" attempts to

clarify the overall meaning and process of salvation.

In this restoration process Christ plays a key role. Christ comes

not only as our mediator but as our example of how to spiritually and

physically live to become God's ideal. Therefore, by uniting our heart

and action with Christ, we are "saved."

The teachings postulate that Jesus was supposed to take a bride and

create the ideal family but his early death limited that plan. The

first Advent brought spiritual salvation and a promise to return. The

Lord of the Second Advent will bring physical salvation. To Church

members, the Second Coming is at hand and Rev. Moon is the prophet whose

revelation and work is preparing the way for Christ's return.

A spiritual world exists as the counterpart of the physical. In

the physical world we mature our spirits, within the limits of time and

BASIC BELIEFS (continued): so that we will be prepared to live with God

   eternally. Heaven is the highest level of the spiritual world where

   perfected people dwell in oneness with God.

AUTHORITATIVE LITERATURE: The Church accepts both Old and New Testament as

   Divine Revelation. The teachings of Rev. Moon, the Divine Principle, are

   largely an interpretation of the Bible, but do include significant

   additional revelation which are given equal authority. The Church also

   publishes many other materials to aid in understanding Rev. Moon's

   revelation, including study guides, condensations of the revelation on

   audio tapes, texts of Rev. Moon's speeches and periodicals.

ETHICAL PRACTICES: Members are expected to keep high moral standards and

   actively witness to their faith, but the only restrictions are on alcohol,

   tobacco and sex outside of the marriage relationship.

HOW DOES THE UNIFICATION CHURCH RECRUIT NEW MEMBERS? The Church recruits by

   direct witnesses, public rallies and the distribution of the Church's

   literature. Generally interested persons attend single lectures and

   later weekend workshops in order to hear the teachings. Membership is

   based on acceptance of the Principles of the Church.

RELATIONSHIP WITH OTHER RELIGIONS: As is indicated by its name, the Church

   strives to work as a catalyst in bringing the religions of the world into

   closer communication and understanding of each other. It is supportive

   of efforts that lead people to God. Rev. Moon and the members of the

   Unification Church see themselves as the fulfillment of Christianity, and

   not contradictory of it.

INTERNATIONAL CHRISTIAN MINISTRIES c/o Duane Pederson Post Office Box 1949 Hollywood, California 90028	Duane Pederson Chaplain AKA: Jesus People

HISTORICAL ROOTS: Founded by Duane Pederson, a former entertainer and Baptist college student, in 1969. Pederson was inspired to publish the Hollywood Free Paper, a free Christian newspaper, after watching a hawker of an underground newspaper on Sunset Boulevard in Hollywood. With the first issue of the Hollywood Free Paper, Christian believers began to band together and started a revival which came to be known as the "Jesus People Movement," first in California and then across the nation. As people were converted, particularly young people, each issue of the paper grew, and Bible study groups, rock music festivals, emergency "hotlines," coffee houses and help for drug abusers developed as part of the work of Jesus People, International, later renamed the International Christian Ministries.

CURRENT WORK LEADER: Rev. Duane Pederson.

ORIGINS IN THE U.S.: (See "Historical Roots.")

NUMBERS OF ADHERENTS IN THE U.S.: Several hundred persons are connected with International Christian Ministries (ICM), but thousands of others have been converted and moved to work in various Christian churches or other parts of the Jesus People movement.

ORGANIZATIONAL STRUCTURE: ICM is organized into a number of ministry centers which find their focus of communication through the Hollywood Free Paper of which Pederson is editor. As leader of the movement, Pederson has ordained and/or commissioned ministers to head the work around the country. Pederson also heads the Jesus People Practicollege.

INTERNATIONAL CHRISTIAN MINISTRIES	Page 2
Leadership, Requirements, Position on Service, Basic Beliefs	

LEADERSHIP AND ROLE OF MINISTERS: Essentially those associated with ministry in traditional evangelical Christianity.

WHO MAY CONDUCT SERVICE? Anyone, but ministers normally lead worship and Bible Studies.

IS GROUP WORSHIP REQUIRED? No, but is strongly encouraged.

WORSHIP REQUIREMENTS: Jesus People gather regularly (several times weekly) for worship, prayer, and Bible Study.

MINIMUM REQUIREMENT FOR WORSHIP: None.

FACILITIES FOR WORSHIP: None.

OTHER SPECIFIC RELIGIOUS REQUIREMENTS OTHER THAN WORSHIP: None (see also "How Does ICM Recruit Members?")

DIETARY LAWS OR RESTRICTIONS: None.

RELIGIOUS HOLIDAYS: Easter and Christmas.

FUNERAL AND BURIAL REQUIREMENTS: None.

AUTOPSY: No restrictions.

CREMATIONS: No restrictions.

UNIFORM APPEARANCE REQUIREMENTS: No restrictions.

POSITION ON SERVICE IN THE ARMED FORCES: None.

IS A PRIEST OR CLERGYPERSON REQUIRED AT TIME OF DEATH? No.

ANY OTHER PRACTICES OR TEACHINGS WHICH MAY CONFLICT WITH MILITARY DIRECTIVES OR PRACTICES: None.

BASIC TEACHINGS OR BELIEFS: International Christian Ministries is at one doctrinally with mainline evangelical Christianity. They believe in Jesus Christ as Savior and Lord and rely on His power to save.

INTERNATIONAL CHRISTIAN MINISTRIES   Page 3

Basic Beliefs, Literature, Ethics, Recruiting, Relationships

BASIC BELIEFS (continued): They teach that God loves each person, but that

man is separated from God because of Sin. In his separated state, he

can neither know nor experience God and new life. Jesus Christ is God's

solution to the problem of separation. Receiving Jesus Christ as Savior

and Lord is the only way to salvation.

They also teach the soon return of Jesus and hence the urgency of

spreading the Gospel.

CREEDAL STATEMENTS AND/OR AUTHORITATIVE LITERATURE: The Jesus People teach

that the Bible is the Word of God and the only authority for faith and

practice. They do, however, distribute and use much literature such as

the Hollywood Free Paper and Duane Pederson's books.

ETHICAL PRACTICES: Essentially those identified in the Scriptures and in

accord with the laws of the land.

HOW DOES ICM RECRUIT MEMBERS? Jesus People see as their major duty the

sharing of their experience of Jesus with others. Their active

evangelical effort is carried on through word-of-mouth, coffee

houses, various service ministries and literature.

RELATIONSHIP WITH OTHER RELIGION: ICM fellowships with Christians of all

evangelical denominations and is active in a variety of churches.

In relation to "nominal" Christians and non-Christians, they are

strongly evangelical, considering personal conversion and commit-

ment to Jesus Christ as a prerequisite to fellowship.

THE MENNONITE CHURCH 528 E. Madison Street Lombard, Illinois 60148	Ivan J. Kauffman General Secretary Mennonite Church General Bd.

HISTORICAL ROOTS: Traced to the Anabaptist Mennonites, originated in Zurich, Switzerland in 1524. Severely persecuted, they spread to areas such as S. Germany and Austria. Among the leaders, most outstanding was Menno Simons (1496-1561), after whom the Mennonites are named.

CURRENT U.S. LEADER: Willis L. Breckbill, Moderator, Mennonite Church General Assembly.

ORIGINS IN THE U.S.: 1st settlement in Germantown, PA, in 1683, by emigrants of Dutch background from Grefeld, Germany. Largest colonial settlement begun in what is now Lancaster County, PA, by Swiss emigrants from Switzerland and the Palatinate, Germany. Daughter colonies established in Virginia, Western Pennsylvania, Ontario, Ohio, and farther west.

NUMBER OF ADHERENTS IN THE U.S.: Approximately 95,000

ORGANIZATIONAL STRUCTURE: The Mennonite Church is established with particular reference to congregations in Canada and the U.S. A General Assembly of 300 delegates meets every 2 years as the official denominational body. Approximately 1,150 congregations are divided into about 20 district conferences throughout the U.S. and Canada. Each congregation is led in its various worship functions by pastors, selected by the congregation.

LEADERSHIP AND ROLE OF PASTORS: In addition to worship leadership, pastors perform baptismal services for receiving new members, lead in communion services, and officiate at marriages and funeral services as requested. Pastors may or may not have formal training in the church colleges or seminaries, and may be selected from the congregation or from outside its membership. Pastors are normally members of Mennonite congregations.

THE MENNONITE CHURCH   Page 2

Worship, Requirements, Position on Service

WHO MAY CONDUCT WORSHIP SERVICES? Any member.

IS GROUP WORSHIP REQUIRED? No (see also "Worship Requirements").

WORSHIP REQUIREMENTS: Members are encouraged to attend a meeting with fellow
    members at least weekly, either in a church building or a member's home.

MINIMUM EQUIPMENT FOR WORSHIP: None.

FACILITIES FOR WORSHIP: None (see also "Worship Requirements").

OTHER SPECIFIC RELIGIOUS REQUIREMENTS OTHER THAN WORSHIP: None.

DIETARY LAWS OR RESTRICTIONS: None.

SPECIAL RELIGIOUS HOLIDAYS: Sundays are regarded as special for worship and
    for observing the resurrection of Jesus Christ from the dead.

FUNERAL AND BURIAL REQUIREMENTS: None.

AUTOPSY: No restrictions.

CREMATION: Individual or family option.

MEDICAL TREATMENT: No restrictions.

UNIFORM APPEARANCE REQUIREMENTS: No required apparel or appearance.

POSITION ON SERVICE IN THE ARMED FORCES: Mennonites believe they should have
    no part in "carnal warfare" or conflict between nations, nor in strife
    between groups, classes, or individuals, and that they should not, there-
    fore, accept military service, either combatant or non-combatant of any
    kind or preparation for such service in any form. This prohibition in-
    cludes labor, money, business, factories, and any other resources, even
    under compulsion. They are urged not to take part in scientific, educa-
    tional, or cultural programs designed to contribute to war, nor in any
    activity that tends to promote ill will or hatred among men or nations.

Position on Service, Basic Beliefs

POSITION ON SERVICE (continued): While they also oppose any form of conscription, they seek ways of serving in wartime and peacetime "through which the demands of the state may be both satisfied and transcended." If war does come, with its destruction, they "willingly render such civilian help as conscience permits, so long as we thereby help to preserve and restore life and not to destroy it." They further declare: "that in wartime, as well as in peacetime, we shall endeavor to continue to live a quiet and peaceable life in all godliness and honesty; avoid joining in the wartime hysteria of hatred, revenge, and retaliation; and manifest a meek and submissive spirit, being obedient to the laws and regulations of the government in all things, including the usual taxes, except when obedience would cause us to violate the teachings of the Scripture and our conscience before God."

IS A PASTOR REQUIRED AT THE TIME OF DEATH? Encouraged, but not required.

ANY OTHER PRACTICES OR TEACHINGS WHICH MAY CONFLICT WITH MILITARY
DIRECTIVE OR PRACTICE: Following Acts 5:29 ("We ought to obey God rather than men."), Mennonites believe that Jesus Christ is ultimate authority, and that any directives from any other human source must not conflict with His commands.

BASIC TEACHINGS OR BELIEFS: The Mennonite "Confession of Faith" states:
(1) We believe in one God eternally existing as Father, Son, and Holy Spirit. (2) We believe that God has revealed Himself in the Scriptures of the Old and New Testaments, the inspired Word of God, and supremely in His Son, the Lord Jesus Christ. (3) We believe that in the beginning

THE MENNONITE CHURCH   Page 4

Basic Beliefs

BASIC BELIEFS (continued): God created all things by His Son. He made man in
the divine image, with free will, moral character, and a spiritual nature.
(4) We believe that man fell into sin, bringing depravity and death upon
the race; that as sinner, man is self-centered and self-willed, unwil-
ling and unable to break with sin. (5) We believe that there is one
Mediator between God and man, the Man Christ Jesus, who died to redeem
us from sin and arose for our justifications. (6) We believe that salvation is by grace through faith in Christ, a free gift bestowed by God
on those who repent and believe. (7) We believe that the Holy Spirit
convicts of sin, effects the new birth, gives guidance in life, empowers
for service, and enables perseverance in faith and holiness. (8) We
believe that the church is the body of Christ, the brotherhood of the
redeemed, a disciplined people obedient to the Word of God, and a
fellowship of love, intercession, and healing. (9) We believe that
Christ commissioned the church to go into all the world, making disciples of all the nations, and ministering to every human need. (10)
We believe it is the will of God that there should be ministers to
teach the Word, to serve as leaders, to administer the ordinances, to
lead the church in the exercises of discipline, and to serve as pastors
and teachers. (11) We believe that those who repent and believe should
be baptized with water as a symbol of baptism with the Spirit, cleansing
from sin, and commitment to Christ. (12) We believe that the church
should observe the communion of the Lord's supper as a symbol of His
broken body and shed blood, and of the fellowship of His church, until

THE MENNONITE CHURCH   Page 5

Basic Beliefs, Ethics

BASIC BELIEFS (continued): His return. (13) We believe in the washing of

the saints' feet as a symbol of brotherhood, cleansing, and service, and

in giving the right hand of fellowship and the holy kiss as symbols of

Christian love. (14) We believe that God has established unique roles

for man and woman, symbolized by man's bared head in praying and prophe-

sying, and by woman's veiled head. (15) We believe that Christian mar-

riage is intended by God to be the union of one man and one woman for

life, and that Christians shall marry only in the Lord. (16) We believe

that Christians are not to be conformed to the world, but should seek to

conform to Christ in every area of life. (17) We believe that Christians

are to be open and transparent in life, ever speaking the truth, and

employing no oaths. (18) We believe that it is the will of God for

Christians to refrain from force and violence in human relations and to

show Christian love to all men. (19) We believe that the state is or-

dained of God to maintain order in society, and that Christians should

honor rulers, be subject to authorities, witness to the state, and pray

for governments. (20) We believe that at death the unsaved enter into

everlasting punishment and the saved into conscious bliss with Christ,

who is coming again, and will raise the dead, sit in judgment, and bring

in God's everlasting kingdom.

CREEDAL STATEMENTS AND/OR AUTHORITATIVE LITERATURE: (See "Basic Teachings.")

ETHICAL PRACTICES: (See "Basic Teachings," especially Numbers 15-18.)

THE MENNONITE CHURCH   Page 6

Recruiting, Relationships

HOW DOES THE MENNONITE CHURCH RECRUIT MEMBERS? Through friendships and other

      forms of witness, people are made aware of the beliefs of the Mennonite

      Church. Interested persons are invited to attend services of the Church

      and in that way are made aware of its beliefs. Those who wish to

      affiliate with the church may apply for membership and are received on

      the basis of their identification with the Christian faith of the Mennon-

      ite Church. The Mennonite Church is a believer's church consisting of

      members who have voluntarily committed themselves to membership and to

      the disciplines of the church.

RELATIONSHIP WITH OTHER RELIGIONS: The Mennonite Church believes in Jesus

      Christ as the way, the truth, and the life. It does not accept other non-

      Christian religions as valid ways to receive eternal life, even though

      those other religions may be the means of accomplishing many good things.

      Cooperation or fellowship with other Christian groups may take place on

      the local level at the option of the Pastor and congregation.

RELIGIOUS SOCIETY OF FRIENDS IN THE U.S. Friends United Meeting 101 Quaker Hill Drive Richmond, Indiana 47374	Lorton G. Heusel General Secretary, Friends United Meeting AKA: Quakers

HISTORICAL ROOTS: Traced to the Society of Friends established by George Fox (1624-1691) in England in approximately 1652, arising out of the Puritan-Reformed movement in 17th Century England.

CURRENT WORLD LEADER: No central organization or leadership. The Friends World Committee for Consultation relates to all groups of Friends and seeks to coordinate Quaker activity and to bring various groups of Friends into dialogue and fellowship.

ORIGINS IN THE U.S.: Because of disorders and religious persecution in England, Quaker immigration began in 1656 to Massachusetts, where many were persecuted, banished or hanged. Quaker settlements were established in many colonies within the next ten years. William Penn obtained a grant of land (Pennsylvania) in 1681 in consideration of a debt the Crown owed his father, Admiral Penn. Penn's "Holy Experiment" accelerated Quaker immigration.

NUMBER OF ADHERENTS IN THE U.S.: Approximately 100,000.

ORGANIZATIONAL STRUCTURE: In Quaker polity, local congregations may be Monthly Meetings or Preparative Meetings. Monthly Meetings, related geographically, comprise a Quarterly or Regional or Area meeting and a larger association of these comprises a Yearly Meeting which is the autonomous and authoritative body. In the U.S., there are 31 Yearly Meetings, 11 of which share in cooperative ministries through the Friends United Meeting, established in 1902. The Friends General Conference, established in 1900, has 10 Yearly meetings, four of which hold membership jointly in Friends United Meeting. Organized in 1966,

RELIGIOUS SOCIETY OF FRIENDS IN THE U.S.	Page 2

Organization, Leadership, Worship

ORGANIZATION (continued): Evangelical Friends Alliance has four Yearly Meetings. Three Yearly Meetings are members of the Conservative group and seven Yearly Meetings are unaffiliated.

LEADERSHIP AND THE ROLE OF MINISTERS AND PASTORS: Friends hold to the universal ministry, believing that every disciple is called to be a minister, though each branch recognizes that some individuals receive a special call to minister. This led to the abolition of the concept of the laity and of professional "priests." In the 1800s, specialized pastoral ministry was recognized in the U.S. and pastors now serve many American Quaker Meetings. Quaker pastors generally have typical Protestant pastoral duties, but their role is that of servant and not authoritative in the sense of conferred power. Since all are ministers, the pastor's task includes encouraging and supporting other members in their ministry. Insofar as there is formal leadership and coordination among those Friends who do not have regular pastors, usually called "unprogrammed" or silent Meetings (Friends), such leadership is exercised by the Clerk (chairman) of each local meeting (congregation) (see also "Worship Requirements.")

WHO MAY CONDUCT SERVICES? Any member.

IS GROUP WORSHIP REQUIRED? No.

WORSHIP REQUIREMENTS: No specific worship requirements, but personal devotional discipline and regular participation in corporate worship is encouraged.

RELIGIOUS SOCIETY OF FRIENDS IN THE U.S.	Page 3

Worship, Requirements, Position on Service

WORSHIP REQUIREMENTS (continued): Many Friends Meetings still hold their
worship Meetings on the basis of silence. Worshipers gather without
a set or planned form of service and individual worshipers, as they are
led by the Spirit, may speak to the Meeting or pray on its behalf (see
also "Leadership").

MINIMUM EQUIPMENT FOR WORSHIP: None.

FACILITIES FOR WORSHIP: Any meeting room.

OTHER SPECIFIC RELIGIOUS REQUIREMENTS OTHER THAN WORSHIP: None.

DIETARY LAWS OR RESTRICTIONS: None (see also "Ethical Practices").

SPECIAL RELIGIOUS HOLIDAYS: None.

FUNERAL AND BURIAL REQUIREMENTS: None.

AUTOPSY: No restrictions.

CREMATION: No restrictions.

MEDICAL TREATMENT: No restrictions.

UNIFORM APPEARANCE REQUIREMENTS: No required apparel or appearance.

POSITION ON SERVICE IN THE ARMED FORCES: Strong historical stand against
participation in armed forces, although individual decision is recognized.
Quakers are essentially non-violent and committed to peaceful resolution
to conflict.

IS A PASTOR OR OTHER REQUIRED AT THE TIME OF DEATH? No.

ANY OTHER PRACTICES OR TEACHINGS WHICH MAY CONFLICT WITH MILITARY DIRECTIVES
OR PRACTICE? Definitely yes! The Quaker vision holds to the ultimate
value and sacredness of human life. Military directives which require

RELIGIOUS SOCIETY OF FRIENDS IN THE U.S.   Page 4

Other Practices, Basic Beliefs

OTHER PRACTICES OR TEACHINGS (continued): training or specific actions in-
    volving the torture or annihilation of other human beings might well cre-
    ate unresolvable conflicts in the minds and hearts of service persons who
    have had Quaker training.

        Furthermore, Quakers are committed in all their decision making to
    the "sense of the Meeting" concept, which holds to the ideal of human
    equality, believing that all have access to the Light (see also "Basic
    Beliefs") and each has something valuable to contribute in determining
    the right course of action. The authoritarian and hierarchial structure
    of the military systems is alien to Quaker beliefs and practices.

BASIC TEACHINGS AND BELIEFS: Friends believe that the source of religious
    authority for both personal and corporate guidance is the Holy Spirit or
    Inner Light of Christ, the Scriptures and religious tradition, along with
    the abiding community of faith. Some might hold one of these to be a
    primary source of authority, while other Friends tend toward another. In
    any case, any one authority needs to be confirmed by the others or at
    least be consistent with the others. They also hold to the universality
    of the Light ("There is a Light that lighteth every man that cometh into
    the world" - John 1:9), which the founder of Quakerism, George Fox, put
    in these terms: "There is that of God in every man." Most Friends be-
    lieve that the observance of the outward *sacraments* is unnecessary; that
    in worship each person may have direct access to the Lord without aid of
    an intermediary.

RELIGIOUS SOCIETY OF FRIENDS IN THE U.S.   Page 5

Basic Beliefs, Literature, Ethics

BASIC BELIEFS (continued): Friends believe in social, economic, interracial

and international justice. They believe that political or governmental

authority is subject to divine authority and that, therefore, the indi-

vidual in matters of conscience must obey God rather than man. Generally,

Friends have held that participation in military service is inconsistent

with their religious principles, and have sought exemption on grounds of

conscience and religious conviction. They recognize, however, that a

consistent policy of non-violence must include a willingness to face per-

sonal risk in administering relief to victims of the tragedy of war and

in performing other non-military service.

CREEDAL STATEMENTS AND/OR AUTHORITATIVE LITERATURE: No one statement or creed

is acknowledged by all Friends.

ETHICAL PRACTICES: No specific standard ethical practices are observed, but

obedience to the Light of Christ within is encouraged.

Total abstinence from narcotics and alcoholic beverages, as well as

tobacco, is encouraged. Friends are urged to abstain from gambling. They

object to oaths, pledges or sworn statements not as a mere negation but

as a positive affirmation of the ideal of utter sincerity and authen-

ticity for the regulation of life and in all one's relationships. A

person's word should be as good as a sworn statement. They discourage

membership in secret organizations.

HOW DO QUAKERS RECRUIT MEMBERS? No specific methods are employed, other than

the encouragement for members (ministers) to share their faith in words

and actions.

RELIGIOUS SOCIETY OF FRIENDS IN THE U.S. Page 6
Relationships
RELATIONSHIP TO OTHER RELIGIONS: (See also "Organizational Structure.") Generally, Quakers cooperate with other Christian bodies and participate in various ecumenical endeavors consistent with their beliefs and practices.

THE REORGANIZED CHURCH OF JESUS CHRIST OF LATTER DAY SAINTS P.O. Box 1059 The Auditorium Independence, Missouri 64051	W. Wallace Smith President AKA: RLDS; Saints Church; "Other Mormons"

HISTORICAL ROOTS: Origin during religious enthusiasm and revival associated with Second Great Awakening in America (early 1800s). Joseph Smith, Jr., with background in Protestant religious tradition, laid claim to "restoration" of First Century Church principles and, based on divine insight and direction, founded movement in Fayette, New York in 1830 to effect the "restoring" of Christ's church in its original form and with its original authority.

CURRENT WORLD LEADERS: The First Presidency, made up of President W. Wallace Smith, grandson of the founder, assisted by two counselors, President Maurice L. Draper and President Duane E. Couey.

ORIGINS IN THE U.S.: Traced to body established by Joseph Smith, Jr. in 1830. Upon Smith's death in Illinois in 1844 various persons made leadership claims and took with them parts of the church, the largest group following Brigham Young to what is now Utah. In 1852, a "new organization" of unattached members began in Wisconsin, and in 1860 Joseph Smith III, son of the founder, accepted leadership of what was to become the Reorganized Church of Jesus Christ of Latter Day Saints. Headquarters were established first in Illinois, then Iowa, and presently in Independence, Missouri.

NUMBER OF ADHERENTS IN THE U.S.: Approximately 220,000.

ORGANIZATIONAL STRUCTURE: World Headquarters Organization includes (1) the First Presidency, the chief executive agency of the church; (2) the Council of the Twelve Apostles, concerned with world-wide missionary activities and administration of the fields under direction of the First

THE REORGANIZED CHURCH OF JESUS CHRIST OF LATTER DAY SAINTS	Page 2

Organization, Leadership

ORGANIZATIONAL STRUCTURE (continued): Presidency; and (3) the Presiding

Bishopric, concerned with church properties, financial matters and stew-

ardship of membership. Directorates, commissions, departments and staff

assist these three major agencies in conducting the spiritual and busi-

ness affairs of the church. Each biennium (2 years) delegates gather for

a World Conference, directed by the First Presidency, and the church's

program and financial affairs are defined by legislative acts of this

body.

LEADERSHIP AND ROLE OF PRIESTHOOD: Various priesthood offices -- deacons,

teachers, priests, elders and high priests -- have specific functions and

responsibilities outlined in the law and practice of the church. High

priests may be called to certain specialized functions within that priest-

hood and thus may function as president, apostle, bishop, and patriarch/

evangelist. Similarly, elders may be called to the specialized function

of Seventy, which is primarily concerned with missionary outreach. The

President of the Church serves as prophet and may from time to time

receive divinely enlightened instructions to the church which became part

of the church's sacred literature, subject to World Conference acceptance.

Priesthood members who become military chaplains, and many who come to

serve as appointees of the church, complete seminary training. Priest-

hood members who do not complete seminary are expected to prepare them-

selves through education and study to be effective wherever called to

serve.

THE REORGANIZED CHURCH OF JESUS CHRIST OF LATTER DAY SAINTS	Page 3
Worship, Requirements	

WHO MAY CONDUCT SERVICES? RLDS chaplains or any member. Administration of certain *sacramental ordinances* (see also "Basic Teachings") is limited to specified priesthood offices.

IS GROUP WORSHIP REQUIRED? No, but it is recommended.

WORSHIP REQUIREMENTS: None, although regular church attendance is considered important. Members in the military are encouraged to participate in local branches and congregations contiguous to military installations. If none are available, then (1) to form denominational study groups, and (2) to attend and support the local military chapel activities. Home family worship (weekly or daily) is encouraged, especially to assist small children into better understanding of Christ, the family and the church.

MINIMUM EQUIPMENT FOR WORSHIP: None, although availability of the Three Standard Books (Bible, Book of Mormon, and Doctrines and Covenants) would be quite important.

FACILITIES FOR WORSHIP: Normally a pulpit, for convenience only, as it is not a requirement.

OTHER SPECIFIC RELIGIOUS REQUIREMENTS OTHER THAN WORSHIP: Present tradition of the church is the practice of closed (members only) Communion; however, military chaplains are authorized to serve Communion without restriction. Members file a *tithing* statement annually and pay *tithing* due, and are expected to share the good news of the restored gospel with friends and neighbors by telling the story and living an exemplary life.

THE REORGANIZATION OF JESUS CHRIST OF LATTER DAY SAINTS	Page 4

Requirements, Position on Service, Basic Beliefs

DIETARY LAWS OR RESTRICTIONS: None, although use of tobacco, alcoholic beverages and non-medicinal drugs is strongly discouraged. Use of these would disqualify member from serving in the priesthood.

SPECIAL RELIGIOUS HOLIDAYS: Christmas and Easter.

FUNERAL AND BURIAL REQUIREMENTS: None.

AUTOPSY: No restrictions.

CREMATION: No restrictions.

MEDICAL TREATMENT: No restrictions. Members frequently call upon elders of the church to provide a special prayer of blessing, known as "administration to the sick." Equal credence is given to benefits of faith and use of medical knowledge.

UNIFORM APPEARANCE REQUIREMENTS: No required apparel or appearance, except the propriety of good taste.

POSITION ON SERVICE IN THE ARMED FORCES: No restrictions. Individual preference is honored, and the church upholds (through official legislative action) the right of *agency,* and will support each member in his/her decision concerning military service.

IS A PRIEST (PRIESTHOOD MEMBER) REQUIRED AT THE TIME OF DEATH? No.

ANY OTHER PRACTICES OR TEACHINGS WHICH MAY CONFLICT WITH MILITARY DIRECTIVES OR PRACTICES? None.

BASIC TEACHINGS AND BELIEFS: Members of the church believe in one God and in God's redeeming grace; in the life, death and resurrection of Jesus Christ; in the ministry of the Holy Spirit; in human worth, freedom,

Basic Beliefs, Literature, Ethics

BASIC TEACHINGS AND BELIEFS (continued): *agency*, and stewardship, in the

   church as a covenant community seeking to embody the ministries of

   Christ in the world; in *ZION* as a concrete implementation of the prin-

   ciples of the kingdom of God on earth, expressed both in present reality

   and future hope; in the call of each person to be a disciple, and in

   the particular call and *ordination* of some to priesthood responsibilities;

   in the *sacramental ordinances* of baptism (by immersion and for persons

   at least eight years old), confirmation, the Lord's Supper (Communion),

   administration to the sick, *ordination*, marriage and special blessing;

   in continuing self-revelation of God and in an open *canon* of scripture.

CREEDAL STATEMENTS AND/OR AUTHORITATIVE LITERATURE: The Bible (The "Inspired

   Version," a revision of the King James translation by Joseph Smith, Jr.,

   is used and accepted. Other translations are commonly used in worship

   and study); Book of Mormon (accepted by the church as having been trans-

   lated by Joseph Smith, Jr., through the "gift and power of God" and

   containing an account of early inhabitants of the American Continent and

   their encounter with Jesus Christ); Doctrine and Covenants (a collection

   of writings primarily coming from the church's presidents, accepted as

   inspired instructions to the present age).

ETHICAL PRACTICES: The church leadership and the biennial World Conferences,

   from time to time, may issue guidelines on various ethical issues which

   are published for the benefit of church members. In general, the

   members are expected to be of high moral character and in good standing

   with their church and community.

THE REORGANIZED CHURCH OF JESUS CHRIST OF LATTER DAY SAINTS	Page 6
Recruiting, Relationships	

HOW DOES THE RLDS CHURCH RECRUIT MEMBERS? The Council of the Twelve Apostles
supervises the Quorums of Seventy (see also "Leadership") and directs
the missionary outreach of the church worldwide, as well as the work of
organizing new missions in other countries and new branches and congregations in the United States. Additionally, each individual church member
feels an obligation to share the good news of the restored gospel with
others. Within a branch or congregation, the pastor will designate a
member (usually in the priesthood) to coordinate these activities and
establish a program of telling the story of the restored gospel to
friends and neighbors.

RELATIONSHIP WITH OTHER RELIGIONS: (See also "Origins in the U.S.") The
church accepts the idea that God works in many different ways or
through many different agencies. In large metropolitan areas, pastors
may join the ministerial alliance and thus participate in community
religious activities. The church does not, however, hold membership
in either the National Council of Churches or the World Council of
Churches.

WATCHTOWER BIBLE AND TRACT SOCIETY
   OF NEW YORK, INC.
117 Adams Street
Brooklyn, New York 11201
	Nathan H. Knorr
	President
	
	AKA: Jehovah's
	        Witnesses

HISTORICAL ROOTS: The original Bible study group was founded in the 1870's by Charles Taze Russell, a Christian minister from Pennsylvania. The Jehovah's Witnesses were sometimes spoken of by others as the Russellites or the Millenial Dawnites, names not now used.

CURRENT PRESIDENT: Mr. Nathan H. Knorr (of international Society).

ORIGINS IN THE U.S.: Zion's Watch Tower Tract Society (Pennsylvania) was first incorporated in 1884, renamed the Watch Tower Bible and Tract Society in 1896, then Watch Tower Bible and Tract Society of Pennsylvania in 1955. The Pittsburgh Bible House served as headquarters from 1889 to 1909. With the incorporation of the People's Pulpit Association (New York), later renamed the Watchtower Bible and Tract Society, Inc. (1939), then the Watchtower Bible and Tract Society of New York, Inc. (1955), the headquarters moved to Bethel Home and the Brooklyn Tabernacle. A third corporation, the International Bible Students Association, was established in England in 1914. Judge Joseph Franklin Rutherford was elected President of the corporations following Russell's death in 1942. In 1931, the name "Jehovah's Witnesses" was specified. In 1942, Nathan Homer Knorr was elected as President of the three corporations.

NUMBER OF ADHERENTS IN THE U.S.: Approximately 550,000.

ORGANIZATIONAL STRUCTURE: (See also "Origins in the U.S.") Jehovah's Witnesses are organized into 97 branches, each of which generally includes one entire nation, around the world. Branches are composed of

WATCHTOWER BIBLE AND TRACT SOCIETY	Page 2
Organization, Leadership, Worship	

ORGANIZATION (continued): districts, districts of circuits, circuits of congregations. In the U.S., there are currently 32 districts and 337 circuits. Each circuit includes approximately 22 congregations.

LEADERSHIP AND THE ROLE OF THE MINISTERS: All trained, baptized and fully
committed Witnesses, men and women, share in giving Bible instruction,
and are called "brother" or "sister" (the terms Reverend and Father are
not used). Women do not baptize, deliver public lectures, or direct men.
Men, women and children are trained at weekly meetings at Kingdom Hall
(see "Facilities for Worship"), and study the Bible and Watchtower
literature at home. Witnesses who spend most of their time witnessing are termed "pioneers."

Congregations are governed by a body of elders appointed by the
governing body in New York. These local ministers (elders) serve without pay. Overseas missionaries and supervisory persons are frequently
full time and are specially trained.

WHO MAY CONDUCT WORSHIP SERVICES? Congregational elders (overseers) appointed
from the Society's headquarters in Brooklyn, New York.

IS GROUP WORSHIP REQUIRED? All are encouraged to attend weekly meetings.

WORSHIP REQUIREMENTS: Before becoming a Witness, one must study the Bible
and learn Christian ways of living. Each is expected to attend several
weekly meetings designed for preparation of effective home missions.
Meetings begin and end with song and prayer. The annual Lord's Evening
Meal, a communion service celebrated on Nisan 14 (usually in late March
or in April) is the only celebration. The majority in attendance

WATCHTOWER BIBLE AND TRACT SOCIETY	Page 3
Worship, Requirements, Position on Service	

WORSHIP REQUIREMENTS (continued): celebrate by their presence, and not

   necessarily by partaking of the bread and wine.

MINIMUM EQUIPMENT FOR WORSHIP: Bible - generally the New World Translation

   of the Holy Scriptures.

FACILITIES FOR WORSHIP: Kingdom Hall, which serves both as place of worship

   and educational center.

OTHER SPECIFIC RELIGIOUS REQUIREMENTS OTHER THAN WORSHIP: Each Witness

   must devote time to spreading the word of Jehovah and the teachings of

   the Bible. Pioneers should spend 90 or more hours each month on this

   task, and special pioneers who are sent to isolated areas and foreign

   countries give a minimum of 140 hours per month.

DIETARY LAWS OR RESTRICTIONS: Consuming of blood and unbled meat is

   prohibited.

SPECIAL RELIGIOUS HOLIDAYS: Nisan 14 (see "Worship Requirements").

FUNERAL AND BURIAL REQUIREMENTS: None.

AUTOPSY: Bodily mutilation for research purposes is discouraged.

CREMATION: Permitted.

MEDICAL TREATMENT: Welcomed, but blood transfusions prohibited.

UNIFORM APPEARANCE REQUIREMENTS: None, except that Witnesses dress neatly.

   in a way that is socially acceptable in the community.

POSITION ON SERVICE IN ARMED FORCES: Refuse to serve in the military of all

   nations, but do not oppose those who do. As "neutrals," Witnesses do

   not join in any wars of the nations.

WATCHTOWER BIBLE AND TRACT SOCIETY   Page 4

Position on Service, Basic Beliefs

IS A MINISTER OR PIONEER REQUIRED AT TIME OF DEATH?   No.

ANY OTHER PRACTICES OF TEACHINGS WHICH MAY CONFLICT WITH MILITARY DIRECTIVES

    OR PRACTICES: Witnesses believe all wordly governments are temporarily

    permitted by God and merit respect. As servants of the Most High God,

    they will not participate in politics or elections and do not serve in

    the military. They respect but do not salute the flag since they be-

    lieve this would be idolatry. They do not accept non-war-related ser-

    vice which may be required as a substitute for military duty.

BASIC TEACHINGS AND BELIEFS: Jehovah's Witnesses believe that the Holy

    Bible is the inspired Word of God, and they follow its counsel closely

    in living clean, meaningful lives, both individually and as families.

    They believe in the one God, Jehovah, and that He sent his firstborn

    Son, Jesus Christ, to earth to ransom sinful mankind from death and to

    restore peace and happiness to mankind through the promised Kingdom.

    The turmoil in the earth since 1914 is a "sign" that the heavenly

    Kingdom is now functioning, and that, within the lifetime of this

    generation, it will destroy the wicked in God's war of Armageddon.

    The survivors and resurrected dead will then enjoy the promised 1,000-

    year reign of Christ and his 144,000 joint heirs, during which time

    paradise will be restored earthwide. On surviving a final test, per-

    fected mankind will enter an eternity of joyful life under the

    loving sovereignty of their God, Jehovah.

WATCHTOWER BIBLE AND TRACT SOCIETY	Page 5

Basic Beliefs, Literature, Ethics

BASIC BELIEFS (continued): Witnesses believe that they must zealously warn the people that Satan's domination of mankind must end shortly in the "great tribulation." They are diligent to teach people through free Bible studies in their homes, making disciples of and baptizing those who are desirous of salvation into God's new order.

CREEDAL STATEMENTS AND/OR AUTHORITATIVE LITERATURE: Witnesses accept the Bible as the infallible word of Jehovah. The New World Translation of the Holy Scriptures, initially released between 1950 and 1960, is generally used. The two periodicals of the Society, The Watchtower and Awake, serve both as a means of keeping Witnesses abreast of the understanding of the Scriptures and as a way of sharing the good news of Jehovah's kingdom.

ETHICAL PRACTICES: No specific set of ethical practices is prescribed by the Jehovah's Witnesses, but it is expected that all will live by Bible principles and seek to further understand the will of the Most High God through continued study. Witnesses are advised to use discretion in selecting movies or television shows. They are to spurn immorality, loose conduct, drugs, smoking and drunkenness, and profane speech. Celebrations which originated in *pagan* traditions, including Christmas, Easter, Halloween and family birthdays are not observed. Those who willfully violate the moral laws of Jehovah as set forth in the Bible may be *disfellowshiped*, if they do not respond when given reproof from the Bible.

WATCHTOWER BIBLE AND TRACT SOCIETY   Page 6

Recruiting, Relationships

HOW DO JEHOVAH'S WITNESSES RECRUIT MEMBERS? Witnesses do not "recruit."
  They do make door-to-door home visits to spread their message and to
  assist people in understanding the Bible. Persons interested in
  Jehovah's Witnesses are offered a warm community which can provide
  comfort and security in a rapidly changing and deteriorating society.
  Educational programs and organizational structures are designed to
  fulfill this promise. Witnesses find security and fellowship in their
  congregational association and learn to treasure their membership in
  this Society above anything offered by the secular world or other
  religions.

RELATIONSHIP WITH OTHER RELIGIONS: Jehovah's Witnesses are totally opposed
  to religious teachings that do not conform to the Bible; but they try
  to be kind and helpful to people of other religions. It is error that
  they hate, not individuals, and it is their objective to show love and
  to do good to all men. The primary purpose of their ministry is seen
  not in the negative sense of seeking to condemn all other religions,
  but in a positive sense, that of helping others to understand and do
  the will of Jehovah, and to find salvation through Christ Jesus.

THE WORLDWIDE CHURCH OF GOD P.O. Box 111 Pasadena, California 91109	Herbert W. Armstrong President and Pastor-General

HISTORICAL ROOTS: The Worldwide Church of God dates to A.D. 31 and the founding of the original Church of God in Jerusalem. However, due to Roman invasion and Roman persecution, the real work of proclaiming the good news lost its momentum by A.D. 70. Over the years, scattered congregations kept the same doctrines and practices of the apostles and kept the same name, the Church of God. Among this remnant were congregations called into being by the advent movement begun by William Miller in the 1840s. They rediscovered the Sabbath, took upon themselves the name, the Church of God, and eventually established a headquarters at Stanberry, Missouri. Mr. Herbert W. Armstrong, the founder of the Worldwide Church of God, was affiliated with this Church of God when he was called to ministry.

CURRENT WORLD LEADERSHIP: Leadership of the Worldwide Church of God is invested in Herbert W. Armstrong, President and Pastor-General, and Garner Ted Armstrong, Executive Vice President.

ORIGINS IN THE U.S.: The Worldwide Church of God (fomerly the Radio Church of God) began in the 1930s in Eugene, Oregon, as a result of the preaching efforts of Herbert W. Armstrong. Mr. Armstrong was ordained as a minister in 1931 by the Oregon Conference of the Church of God (7th Day) located at Stanberry, Missouri. In 1933, another Church of God (7th Day) was formed at Salem, West Virginia. Mr. Armstrong was chosen as one of 70 elders. Under his leadership, the Radio Church of God was connected with the Salem Church of God (7th Day) until

THE WORLDWIDE CHURCH OF GOD   Page 2

Origins, Organization, Leadership

ORIGINS (continued): about the year 1937, when his involvement with that
     group was terminated. The Radio Church of God went on the air in
     January, 1934, and commenced publishing the Plain Truth magazine in
     February of that year. In 1947, Ambassador College was founded in
     Pasadena, California. The headquarters were also moved to Pasadena,
     and in 1968 the name was changed from Radio Church of God to Worldwide
     Church of God.

NUMBER OF ADHERENTS IN THE U.S.: As of 1976, there were approximately
     60,000 members in over 200 congregations. The Plain Truth magazine
     circulates over a million copies worldwide.

ORGANIZATIONAL STRUCTURE: Authority in the Worldwide Church of God is ex-
     ercised by Herbert W. Armstrong through his calling as an apostle.
     Assisting him is the Vice President, Garner Ted Armstrong. In the
     United States there are 13 area coordinators, each responsible to the
     Pasadena headquarters. They in turn oversee the work of the elders
     (pastors) of the congregations.

LEADERSHIP AND ROLE OF ELDERS OR MINISTERS: Each local congregation of the
     Worldwide Church of God has as its leader either an elder (the lowest
     rank of the ministry) who serves the group but supports himself with
     outside income, or a college-trained minister who is ordained from
     headquarters.

     Generally several congregations in the same geographic area are
     looked after--in terms of finances, social needs, etc.--by a

THE WORLDWIDE CHURCH OF GOD   Page 3

Leadership, Worship, Holidays

LEADERSHIP (continued): designated pastor. In addition, coordination of

   congregations is also done on a regional basis across several states.

WHO MAY CONDUCT WORSHIP SERVICES? Ordained ministers or designated local

   elders.

IS GROUP WORSHIP REQUIRED? Yes, every Sabbath. The Sabbath begins at sun-

   set on Friday and continues through sunset on Saturday.

WORSHIP REQUIREMENTS: On the Sabbath, members must rest from their labors,

   following the commands and example of the apostle Paul, the New Testa-

   ment Church, and Jesus (see also "Special Religious Holidays").

MINIMUM EQUIPMENT FOR WORSHIP: None.

FACILITIES FOR WORSHIP: Nothing special.

OTHER SPECIFIC RELIGIOUS REQUIREMENTS OTHER THAN WORSHIP: None.

DIETARY LAWS OR RESTRICTIONS: Members of the Church follow the dietary laws

   laid down in Deuteronomy 14 and Leviticus 11 in which certain foods are

   designated "unclean" and hence not eaten. Such unclean foods include

   pork, meat from strangled animals, clams, oysters, etc.

SPECIAL RELIGIOUS HOLIDAYS: The Worldwide Church of God keeps the annual

   festivals as given to ancient Israel by God and recorded in Leviticus

   23. The exact days of the Holy Days will vary from year-to-year on

   the Gregorian calendar, as they are figured on the Hebrew calendar.

   The festivals are: First Day of the Sacred Year - Nisan 1; Passover -

   Nisan 14 (late March or early April); Days of Unleavened Bread - Nisan

   15-21; Pentecost - May or June; Feast of Trumpets - Tishri 1 (September

THE WORLDWIDE CHURCH OF GOD   Page 4

Requirements, Position on Service

HOLIDAYS (continued): or October); Day of Atonement - Tishri 10; Feast of

Tabernacles - Tishri 15-21; and The Last Great Day - immediately follows

the Feast of Tabernacles.

During the Feast of Unleavened Bread, members gather on the first

and last days at designated Festival sites around the United States.

They also eat no leavening during this time. Meetings are also held on

each of the other annual Holy Days.

FUNERAL AND BURIAL REQUIREMENTS: None.

AUTOPSY: No restrictions.

CREMATION: No restrictions.

MEDICAL TREATMENT: No restrictions other than those of the individual's con-

science involving divine healing.

UNIFORM APPEARANCE REQUIREMENTS: No restrictions.

POSITION ON SERVICE IN THE ARMED FORCES: Members of the Worldwide Church of

God believe that Christian disciples are forbidden by Christ and the

commandments of God to kill, or in any way directly or indirectly to

take human life; that bearing arms is directly contrary to this funda-

mental doctrine of belief; and therefore they refuse conscientiously to

bear arms or to come under the military authority.

IS AN ELDER OR MINISTER REQUIRED AT TIME OF DEATH? No.

ANY OTHER PRACTICES OR TEACHINGS WHICH MAY CONFLICT WITH MILITARY DIRECTIVES

OR PRACTICES: (See "Position on Service in the Armed Forces.")

Basic Beliefs, Literature

BASIC TEACHINGS OR BELIEFS: The Worldwide Church of God believes in God, the
Messiahship of Jesus, the Holy Spirit, God's revelation in the Old and
New Testament, the personality of Satan, and man created in the image
of God.

Further the Church believes that through Adam's sin, and through
each individual's transgression of God's law, all men become sinners and
under the penalty of death. God sent Jesus as the representative and
substitutionary sacrifice, thus making it possible for God to forgive
man's sin. Christ was crucified on a Wednesday and resurrected on a
Saturday.

The Church teaches that the ten lost tribes of Israel (House of
Israel) migrated to northwest Europe and Great Britain where decendants
today represent the House of Israel in prophecy.

The Church observes the memorial supper, instituted by Christ, on
the 14th of Nisan. The memorial supper includes footwashing and the
eating of bread (unleavened) and wine. Christmas, Easter, Lent, Valen-
tine's Day, Halloween, and birthdays are not celebrated, but Thanksgiving may be observed.

Two *tithes* are required of Church members. One *tithe* is paid to
the church annually. A second *tithe* is retained by the member and
used at the annual festivals.

CREEDAL STATEMENTS AND/OR AUTHORITATIVE LITERATURE: The Worldwide Church of
God believes the Scriptures of the Old and New Testaments are the

THE WORLDWIDE CHURCH OF GOD	Page 6

Literature, Ethics, Recruitment, Relationships

LITERATURE (continued): complete expressed will of God to man, and are the
supreme and final authority in faith and life.

The Church publishes numerous booklets, a correspondence course,
and the Plain Truth magazine which aid in understanding the Bible and
Church teachings.

ETHICAL PRACTICES: Sin is the transgression of the law, and hence the Church
members strive to keep the Law as summed up in the word "Love." Love
involves the two great principles of love to God and love to neighbor,
and the Ten Commandments compose the ten points of the Law.

HOW DOES THE WORLDWIDE CHURCH OF GOD RECRUIT NEW MEMBERS? The Worldwide
Church of God has an extensive national and international radio and TV
ministry and circulates millions of pieces of literature annually.
Members also, by word-of-mouth, witness to their faith.

RELATIONSHIP WITH OTHER RELIGIONS: The Worldwide Church of God believes that,
as the true Church of God consisting of those believers who are being
led by the Holy Spirit, they have a mission to preach the Gospel of the
coming Kingdom of God to all nations and to reach and reconcile to God
such people as are now called.

INTRODUCTION: INDIAN HERITAGE GROUPS

India is the home of the world's oldest major religious heritage, Hinduism. In its oldest forms, Hinduism is pre-historic in origin, but has undergone numerous developments, attempted reforms, and changes due to varying local pressures. The history of Hinduism begins with the Indo-European Invasion of India in waves dating to 5000 B.C. During this period the Rig-Veda, the oldest of India's sacred books, was written. The faith was a vigorous, worldly religion with a very positive view of the after-life.

The second stage of Hindu history centers on the production of the Upanishads, the major collection of Hindu religious writings, and the rise of the ruling Brahman class. During this period, beginning about 1000 B.C., a change from the positive attitudes of the Vedic period to a generally pes-simistic view of life occurred, and the ideas of karma and reincarnation came to the fore. Reincarnation, the concept that a person may go through a suc-cession of earthly lives, in its more extreme forms, teaches that a soul may return as an animal or even a plant. The rationale for reincarnation is karma, the principle of retribution, a law of justice which brings upon in-dividuals the inevitable consequences of their actions.

Escape from karma and the wheel of reincarnation is by absorbtion into Brahma, the world soul. This absorbtion is most frequently accomplished by practicing yoga, a discipline designed to lead first to self-integration and then integration with Brahma.

There are four main groups of yoga disciplines--bhakti, jnana, karma, and raja. (What is commonly taught in the United States as yoga, hatha

exercises, is not technically yoga, but pre-yoga exercises for body integration prior to practicing yoga.) Bhakti yoga is the way to God through
devotional service. Jnana is the discipline of ideas and knowledge. Karma
is work, and raja or royal yoga approaches Brahma through meditative exercises
The types of yoga are to accommodate the different types of individuals --
emotional, scholarly, active and mystical. Besides the four main types, there
are numerous techniques such as japa yoga which involves the repetition of one
or more words (termed "mantrum") over and over again. Other yogas go under
the names prana, kriya, siddha, and integral.

During the Brahmic period, the several major schools of Hinduism, each
related to different aspects of Brahma (dieties), emerged. The Vaishnavas
worship Krishna as the primary aspect of Brahma. As a whole they follow
Patanjali, the ancient teacher of yoga. A third group follow Shakti, Siva's
female consort, often called "Kundalini."

The Brahmic era was disrupted by the conquest of India by Great Britian.
An initial defensive reaction to British rule and Christian missions was followed by the creative Hindu Renaissance, the third stage of Hindu development.
Led by a number of outstanding leaders such as Ram Mohan Roy and Sri Ramakrishna, reformed Hindu movements emerged. Almost all American Hindu groups
represent either older groups which have been restructured by the Renaissance or new groups produced by it. The International Society for Krishna
Consciousness represents the former and the Divine Light Mission the latter.

Hinduism's history in America dates to 1893 and the appearance of several
spokesmen at the Parliament of Religions in Chicago. Swami Vivekananda, a

disciple of Ramakrishna, became a nationally known figure because of his ora-
torical ability and vibrant personality. After the Parliament he established
the Vedanta Society, America's first Hindu group. Over the years, several
Hindu teachers came to the United States, most notably Swami Yogananda, who
founded the Self-Realization Society. Only after World War II, however, did
Hinduism begin to make a major impact. The growth of modern Hinduism was made
possible by the increased study of comparative religion in colleges and uni-
versities, the cross-fertilization occasioned by American visitors to India,
and the increasing number of Gurus (i.e., teachers) who migrated and settled
in America.

Currently, there is some controversy regarding transcendental meditation
(TM). Asserting that TM is not a religion, the World Plan Executive Council
has accepted large grants to teach TM in the public schools and armed forces.
A group claiming that transcendental meditation is in fact a religion has
arisen to challenge the Council's status. They contend that because of the
historical use of japa yoga, the initiation ceremony which includes prayers to
Vishnu and Siva, and the theology implicit in the "Science of Creative Intelligence," TM is in fact a religion and the World Plan Executive Council a
religious body. The resolution of this controversy, including any related
court actions, will have a future impact on TM.

The three groups included in this section are among some fifty Indian
Heritage bodies in the United States. Though the three are among the most
successful, none of them are Sivaites or Shaktites as most Hindu bodies are.

DIVINE LIGHT MISSION P. O. Box 532 Denver, Colorado 80201	Mr. Joe Anctil Public Information Department International Headquarters

HISTORICAL ROOTS: Divine Light Mission was first founded in India in 1960 by
Shri Hans Ji Maharaj. Following his death, Shri Hans Ji appointed the
youngest of his four sons, Sant Ji, as the next Perfect Master and thereby he assumed head of Divine Light Mission as decreed by his father.
Since that time, Guru Maharaj Ji has inspired a worldwide movement and
the Mission is active in approximately 55 countries.

CURRENT WORLD LEADER: Spiritual Master of the Divine Light Mission is Guru
Maharaj Ji.

ORIGINS IN THE U.S.: On November 8, 1970, Maharaj Ji proclaimed his Mission
to the western part of the world, and early the following year he departed India for a tour that brought him to the United states. Divine Light
Mission was formally established in the United States in 1971 as a
religious organization and later was recognized as a church by the United
States Government in 1974.

NUMBER OF ADHERENTS IN THE U.S.: 50,000 involved; 10,000 to 12,000 very
active.

ORGANIZATIONAL STRUCTURE: The Spiritual Head of the International movement
is Guru Maharaj Mi. The U.S. Mission, which is incorporated and head-
quartered in the State of Colorado, is managed by a Board of Directors
which supervises the activities of its twenty-three branches located
throughout the U.S.

LEADERSHIP AND ROLE OF MINISTERS: The Ministers of Divine Light Mission
(often called Initiators or Mahatmas) are spiritual heads of Divine
Light Mission Communities throughout the world. A large number of the

DIVINE LIGHT MISSION   Page 2

Leadership, Worship

LEADERSHIP (continued): Ministers are missionaries who travel continuously

   around the world. All of the Ministers conduct their church duties,

   which, being consistent with the spiritual teachings of Guru Maharaj Ji,

   include the initiation of interested persons into the experience, the

   teaching of meditation as a means of self-realization and the giving

   of spiritual discourses.

WHO MAY CONDUCT SERVICES?: Spiritual discourses or services (hereafter called

   satsang), meditation and service are the fundamental activities of the

   church. Ministers are the only members authorized to teach meditation.

   However, any Community Coordinator formally appointed by Divine Light

   Mission in any given city or township is authorized to conduct formal

   satsang programs nightly. In extreme situations where there is no formal

   community, two or more members are encouraged to hold nightly discourse,

   as this activity is a prerequisite of the church. Any member of Divine

   Light Mission while serving in the Armed Forces may receive special

   permission from National Headquarters or the nearest Community Coordin-

   ator to conduct and coordinate the services required by the church on

   Military Installation.

IS GROUP WORSHIP REQUIRED? Daily meditation and nightly satsang are required

   activities for each member.

WORSHIP REQUIREMENTS: Each member is required to meditate formally twice

   daily and to attend spiritual discourses (satsang) nightly.

MINIMUM EQUIPMENT FOR WORSHIP: Though not required, many meditators use a

   blanket to cover themselves while meditating, to shut out disturbances

DIVINE LIGHT MISSION	Page 3
Worship, Requirements	

MINIMUM EQUIPMENT (continued): and to conceal secret meditation techniques.

   They might also use a baragon, a "T" shaped tool to aid in technique.

FACILITIES FOR WORSHIP: Each of the branches maintains a center for this pur-

   pose and frequently services are held within members' homes. A private

   quiet room is necessary for meditation.

OTHER SPECIFIC REQUIREMENTS FOR WORSHIP: Each member is encouraged to do

   Service, which means to perform activities from an experience of devotion

   and meditation for Divine Light Mission, such as *tithing* 10 percent of his

   or her income.

DIETARY LAWS OR RESTRICTIONS: Most members are encouraged to be vegetarians,

   but this is a personal choice. If a member is in the Monastic Order or a

   Minister, then he or she must refrain from eating meat, fish or eggs.

SPECIAL RELIGIOUS HOLIDAYS: There are three special religious holidays which

   are observed by all members of Divine Light Mission and last for one full

   week or seven days duration. All members must attend these holidays if

   it is at all possible. They are of great significance in an individual's

   spiritual growth and for an active member they are mandatory. These are

   in March (Holi Festival), in July (Guru Paja), and in November (Hans

   Jayanti). There are some unscheduled programs from time to time that are

   decided upon by Guru Maharaj Ji and members are expected to attend.

   Members of Divine Light Mission also partake in the religious programs

   of their families' faith at their own discretion.

FUNERAL AND BURIAL REQUIREMENTS: None.

AUTOPSY: No restrictions.

DIVINE LIGHT MISSION   Page 4

Position on Service, Basic Beliefs, Literature, Ethics, Recruiting

CREMATION: Permitted.

MEDICAL TREATMENT: No restrictions.

UNIFORM APPEARANCE REQUIREMENTS: None.

POSITION ON SERVICE IN THE ARMED FORCES: A matter of individual preference.

IS A PRIEST OR CLERGY PERSON REQUIRED AT TIME OF DEATH? No.

ANY OTHER PRACTICES OR TEACHINGS WHICH MAY CONFLICT WITH MILITARY DIRECTIVES
     OR PRACTICES: None.

BASIC TEACHINGS OR BELIEFS: Divine Light Mission was organized to facili-
     tate the teachings of Guru Maharaj Ji. Guru Maharaj Ji reveals Knowl-
     edge, which itself cannot be adequately described in words but which
     can be experienced deeply through satsang, service and meditation, the
     fundamental practices of this worship.

CREEDAL STATEMENTS AND/OR AUTHORITATIVE LITERATURE: The teachings of
     Guru Maharaj Ji given in satsang programs have special authority
     and meaning to all members and are circulated and read throughout
     the membership. The two periodicals Elan Vital and Divine Times
     and films and tapes are the major organs for publishing His teachings.

ETHICAL PRACTICES: There are no ethical practices in terms of rules and
     norms. Members believe that involvement in satsang, service and medita-
     tion is a living code which dispells inner conflict and leaves the
     individual at peace.

HOW DOES DIVINE LIGHT MISSION RECRUIT MEMBERS? The Mission holds intro-
     ductory programs but most persons come to the Mission through their
     acquaintances with other members.

DIVINE LIGHT MISSION	Page 5

Relationships

RELATIONSHIP WITH OTHER RELIGIONS: There is no conflict between the Divine

   Light Mission and other faiths. The teachings of Guru Maharaj Ji involve

   the member in an experience, not a belief, according to the Mission.

THE INTERNATIONAL SOCIETY FOR KRISHNA CONSCIOUSNESS Regional Headquarters 10310 Oaklyn Road Potomac, Maryland 20854	Rupanuga das Adhikari, Regional Secretary Governing Body Commission AKA: Hare Krishna Movement or American Krishna Movement

HISTORICAL ROOTS: Krishna consciousness means to be conscious of God. It is recorded in the Vedic scriptures (Veda means knowledge), many of which are acknowledged to be at least 5,000 years old (3,000 B.C.) in written history alone. Previous to 3,000 B.C. there was a disciplic succession of spiritual masters who passed on Krishna consciousness and this disciplic succession continues until the present day. Historically, the Movement is known as the Vaishnava religion. Vaishnava means personal servant of God, the same God of the Bible and Koran. The modern spread of Vaishnavism outside of India was first due to the inspiration and teachings of Lord Chaitanya Mahaprabhu (1486-1534 A.D.) which were later taken up in the mid-19th century by Bhaktivinode Thakur, who translated Vaishnava works intended for the English-speaking countries. The Thakur's disciple was Bhaktisiddhanta Saraswati, the spiritual master of the world leader of the movement.

CURRENT WORLD LEADER: His Divine Grace A.C. Bhaktivedanta Swami Prabhupada (Srila Prabhupada).

ORIGINS IN THE U.S.: Srila Prabhupada came to the United States in 1965, having been especially commissioned by his spiritual master to bring Krishna consciousness to the Western countries, and founded the International Society for Krishna Consciousness (ISKCON) in New York City the following year. There he began publishing Back to Godhead, the Society's monthly periodical.

NUMBER OF ADHERENTS IN THE U.S.: The Movement has 2,500 monks, priests and and ministerial students (including women) and a 250,000 member lay

Organization, Leadership

ADHERENTS (Continued): congregation. This approximate number is arrived at

   by counting each person who visits an ISKCON facility at least once per

   month as a congregation member.

ORGANIZATIONAL STRUCTURE: ISKCON was founded by and is headed by Srila

   Prabhupada, its spiritual leader. He is assisted by a number of

   regional representatives or secretaries. Each such representative over-

   sees a portion of the approximately 108 local centers in operation

   world-wide. Each local temple is self-sufficient.

LEADERSHIP AND THE ROLE OF MINISTERS: A president, discipled by Srila

   Prabhupada, serves each local facility as its spiritual leader and

   administrator. (A disciple means one initiated by the spiritual master

   and who accepts vows outlined below.)

        Currently, there are five functioning orders within the Society:

   three are classifications based on spiritual criteria and two, on

   functional criteria. Of the three spiritual orders, the first includes

   neophyte men (brahmacaries) and women (brahmacarinis) who are unmarried.

   Analogies for these men and women in the first spiritual order would be

   monks and nuns. If they choose to get married, they become grhasthas,

   the second order. If the men choose to stay celibate, they can even-

   tually achieve the third order, called sannyas, which is the highest

   order and demands a permanent vow of celibacy.

        In addition, there are two other orders which relate to the kind

   of work or service performed by members of the Society. The first is

   the "priestly class" or brahmins, who function as priests (pujaris),

KRISHNA CONSCIOUSNESS   Page 3

Leadership, Worship

LEADERSHIP (continued): teachers, and administrators. The second is the

    business or farming class, the vaisyas, who are engaged in the produc-

    tion of foodstuffs and in the protection of cows in various projects.

        All members, no matter which order they are in, receive a second

    initiation from the spiritual master which is a further commitment to

    keep the previous vows without fail. Ultimately, all devotees are

    designated as Vaishnavas, but to extend the Movement, the Society is

    organized into such divisions of labor and levels of spiritual develop-

    ment, as described above.

WHO MAY CONDUCT SERVICES? In the Temple, the brahmins (second initiates)

    are responsible for worship, instruction, ceremonies, etc., and are

    expected to preach.

IS GROUP WORSHIP REQUIRED? Yes, at least twice a day for full disciples.

WORSHIP REQUIREMENTS: Each devotee is required to arise before sunrise for

    worship and chanting. The program includes chanting the holy names of

    God before the Deities (representations of the Supreme Being and pure

    devotees or saints, similar to the images often utilized in Catholic

    Churches and not to be confused with so-called "idol-worshiping").

    The evening ceremony is similar.

MINIMUM EQUIPMENT FOR WORSHIP: Japa (prayer) beads, kunti or sacred bead

    necklace and telok (marking on the forehead).

FACILITIES FOR WORSHIP: Worship is normally performed in a Temple with an

    altar, Deities and a seat for the spiritual master.

OTHER SPECIFIC RELIGIOUS REQUIREMENTS OTHER THAN WORSHIP: (See "Dietary Laws"

KRISHNA CONSCIOUSNESS	Page 4

Requirements, Position Service

RELIGIOUS REQUIREMENTS (continued): and "Ethical Practices.")

DIETARY LAWS AND/OR REQUIREMENTS: Devotees eat no fish, meat, eggs, garlic,

   or onions. Alcohol, drugs, coffee, tea, and smoking are not permitted.

RELIGIOUS HOLIDAYS: All holidays of the ISKCON are reckoned according to

   the lunar calendar, and occur on different days each year. The eleventh

   day after the full moon each month (called Ekadaski) is a fast day from

   beans and grains. The annual calendar begins in the spring on the birth-

   day of Lord Chaitanya (March or April). The major festivals are: Jagan-

   natha or Rathayatra (July); Janamastami, Kirshna's Birthday (August) and

   Vyasa Puja, the spiritual master's birthday (August).

FUNERAL AND BURIAL REQUIREMENTS: None.

AUTOPSY: No restrictions.

CREMATION: Generally encouraged.

MEDICAL TREATMENT: Devotees use customary medical treatment, but prefer

   herbal or natural treatments to any use of antibiotics.

UNIFORM AND APPEARANCE REQUIREMENTS: Each male devotee wears a sikha, a tuft

   of hair, and usually no more than a month's growth of hair. After bath-

   ing, telok or clay is marked twelve places on the body, each represent-

   ing a name of God. Most noticeable are the two white parallel lines of

   telok on the forehead, coming to a V-shaped point at the bridge of the

   nose (the traditional symbol of a Vaishnava).

POSITION ON SERVICE IN THE ARMED FORCES: Devotees are non-violent. On the

   basis of full-time devotional service, devotees have sought draft-exempt

   status as ministerial students on an individual basis.

Position on Service, Basic Beliefs

IS A PRIEST REQUIRED AT TIME OF DEATH? Yes, if at all possible. Otherwise,
the blessings of a qualified priest are not required for a person to go
back to Godhead.

ARE THERE ANY PRACTICES OR TEACHINGS WHICH MAY CONFLICT WITH MILITARY
DIRECTIVES? The lifestyle and religious practices of a full-time devotee preclude time for service in the military, in much the same way
that a divinity student's schedule might.

BASIC BELIEFS: 1. By sincerely cultivating a bona fide spiritual science,
we can be free from anxiety and come to a state of pure, unending, bliss-
ful consciousness in this lifetime. 2. We are not our bodies but eternal
spirit souls, parts and parcels of God (Krishna). As such, we are all
brothers, and Krishna is ultimately our common father. 3. Krishna is
the eternal, all-knowing, omnipresent, all-powerful, and all-attractive
Personality of Godhead. He is the seed-giving father of all living beings and He is the sustaining energy of the entire cosmic creation. 4.
The Absolute Truth is contained in all the great scriptures of the world.
However, the oldest known revealed scriptures in existence are the Vedic
literatures, most notably the Bhagavad-gita, which is the literal record
of God's actual words. 5. We should learn the Vedic knowledge from a
genuine spiritual master - one who has no selfish motives and whose mind
is firmly fixed on Krishna. 6. Before we eat, we should offer to the
Lord the food that sustains us. Then Krishna becomes the offering and
purifies us. 7. We should perform all our actions as offerings to
Krishna and do nothing for our own sense gratification. 8. The

Basic Beliefs, Literature, Ethics, Recruiting, Relationships

BASIC BELIEFS (continued): recommended means for achieving the mature stage

of love of God in this age of Kali, or quarrel, is to chant the holy

names of the Lord. The easiest method for most people is to chant the

Hare Krishna mantra: Hare Krishna, Hare Krishna, Krishna Krishna, Hare

Hare. Hare Rame, Hare Rama, Rama Rama, Hare Hare.

CREEDAL STATEMENTS AND/OR AUTHORITATIVE LITERATURE: The Absolute Truth is

contained in all the great Scriptures of the world, the Bible, the Koran

the Torah, etc., and the oldest known revealed Scriptures are the Vedic

literatures.

ETHICAL PRACTICES: Regulative Principles: 1) no illicit sex; 2) no gambling;

3) no intoxication of any kind, including coffee, tea, and cigarettes;

and 4) no eating of meat, fish, eggs.

HOW DOES THE SOCIETY RECRUIT MEMBERS? Krishna Consciousness is offered to

the public through the chanting of God's names, the distribution of

foodstuffs first offered to God, and the distribution of literature

(30 languages).

RELATIONSHIP WITH OTHER RELIGIONS: ISKCON recognizes those religions based

upon the recognized Scriptures of the world. Vaishnavas adopt the non-

sectarian view that religion means to surrender to God, follow the laws

of God (e.g., the Ten Commandments), and revive the love for God dormant

in the hearts of all. The test of real religion is whether these tenets

are achieved, i.e., God is One and therefore religion is also one.

WORLD PLAN EXECUTIVE COUNCIL 17310 Sunset Blvd. Pacific Palisades, California 90272	Mr. John Konhause National Board AKA: Transcendental Meditation: TM

HISTORICAL ROOTS: The Transcendental Meditation (TM) program features the use of the TM technique, a newly rediscovered method for expanding the use of the mind and refining the physiology to the extent that it can support the neurophysiological state of enlightenment. The introduction of the technique was the work of an Indian scholar and teacher, Maharishi Mahesh Yogi, who did not invent the technique, but rather, revived it. Maharishi's special contribution is not only in making the TM technique available for the first time to large numbers of people in the world, but also in making it available in a form suitable for precise objective investigation. Studies have verified many physiological, phychological, and sociological benefits from the TM technique.

CURRENT WORLD LEADERSHIP: The International Association for the Advancement of the Science of Creative Intelligence supervises the Transcendental Meditation movement's activities throughout the world. The association is a nonprofit organization which acts through a Board of Directors. On teaching-related matters, it receives guidance from Maharishi.

ORIGINS IN THE U.S.: In 1959, Maharishi began teaching the TM technique to individuals throughout the world, and for several years remained the only teacher. He began a series of courses in 1966 to train TM teachers in order that the technique could be made available more widely.

NUMBER OF PERSONS PRACTICING THE TM TECHNIQUE: Over 900,000 persons have taken the basic TM course in the United States alone.

ORGANIZATIONAL STRUCTURE: In the U.S., World Plan Executive Council (a non-profit, educational corporation) is responsible for supervising the

WORLD PLAN EXECUTIVE COUNCIL   Page 2

Organization, Leadership

ORGANIZATIONAL STRUCTURE (continued): activities of the TM movement. There

    are now over 7,000 TM teachers and about 400 teaching centers located

    throughout the U.S. The organization offers instruction in the TM tech-

    nique but the individuals who receive such instruction need not devote

    time to furthering the growth of the organization. In addition to the

    World Plan Executive Council, there is a four-year liberal arts univers-

    ity in Fairfield, Iowa. Maharishi International University (a separate

    corporation) offers the traditional academic disciplines from the uni-

    fying perspective of the Science of Creative Intelligence, the theore-

    tical framework for study of the origin and growth of creative intelli-

    gence in the individual and in the environment (see "Basic Teachings.")

LEADERSHIP AND ROLE OF TEACHERS:. The TM movement is staffed primarily by vol-

    unteers who usually receive a very small salary or living stipend. Gen-

    erally a person becomes involved in the movement after personally ex-

    periencing the benefits of the TM technique.

        The role of the TM teacher is to teach the TM technique itself and

    to provide intellectual understanding about the meditators' experiences

    during the practice of the technique. Requirements for becoming a tea-

    cher include firsthand knowledge about the TM technique through medita-

    tion as well as the information presented during the extensive training

    program all TM teachers must complete over a period of several months.

    All persons who become qualified as TM teachers teach the technique in

    the same way, ensuring that the effectiveness of the technique is not

WORLD PLAN EXECUTIVE COUNCIL   Page 3

Leadership, Worship, Requirements, Position on Service

LEADERSHIP (continued): diluted due to any individual differences of the

teachers.

Teachers present introductory programs, teach the basic TM course,

and offer follow-up programs and weekend residential courses. (A TM

Club has been established in the Pentagon.)

WHO MAY LEAD TM ACTIVITIES? Qualified teachers conduct courses and follow-up

events. Individual meditation is practiced alone.

ARE GROUP SESSIONS REQUIRED? No, once the basic technique is learned.

PARTICIPATION REQUIREMENTS: Fifteen to 20 minutes twice a day.

MINIMUM EQUIPMENT FOR MEDITATION: None.

FACILITITES FOR MEDITATION: None.

OTHER TM REQUIREMENTS OTHER THAN MEDITATION: None. Further participation

(including follow-up meetings and "checkings") is optional.

DIETARY LAWS OR RESTRICTIONS: None.

SPECIAL DAYS OF SIGNIFICANCE: None, although special awards are presented

at quarterly celebrations.

FUNERAL AND BURIAL REQUIREMENTS: None.

AUTOPSY: No restrictions.

CREMATION: No restrictions.

MEDICAL TREATMENT: No restrictions.

UNIFORM APPEARANCE REQUIREMENTS: None.

POSITION ON SERVICE IN THE ARMED FORCES: None.

IS A LEADER OR TEACHER REQUIRED AT TIME OF DEATH? No.

WORLD PLAN EXECUTIVE COUNCIL   Page 4

Basic Beliefs

ANY OTHER PRACTICES OR TEACHINGS WHICH MAY CONFLICT WITH MILITARY DIRECTIVES

 OR PRACTICES: None.

BASIC TEACHINGS OR BELIEFS: The World Plan Executive Council offers teach-

 ings in two areas: theoretical (The Science of Creative Intelligence,

 or SCI) and practical (the Transcendental Meditation, or TM, program).

 SCI was founded upon the basis of the practice of the TM technique,

 the means for regularly contacting the limitless source of energy and

 intelligence within.

  Not a religion, philosophy, or belief system, the TM technique is

 an effortless, automatic procedure for allowing the mind gradually to

 settle down until the least excited state of mind is reached. This is

 a state of inner wakefulness, of pure consciousness aware of its own un-

 bounded nature. It is wholeness, beyond the division of subject and

 object--transcendental consciousness. It is a field of all possibilities,

 where all creative potentialities exist. It is a state of perfect order,

 the matrix from which all the laws of nature emerge, the source of crea-

 tive intelligence.

  The mind is able to reach this state quite naturally and effortlessly

 due to a tendency inherent in the human thinking process. Thus the tech-

 nique works automatically for everyone who learns it in the proper

 way. No intellectual understanding is required because the TM tech-

 nique is not an intellectual practice. As the mind reaches this

 least excited state, the activity of the nervous system also settles

WORLD PLAN EXECUTIVE COUNCIL   Page 5

Basic Beliefs

BASIC BELIEFS (continued): down to an unprecedented level of rest, allowing

deeply rooted stresses to be released, which strengthens the entire

system.

Through the regular alternation of the TM technique with activity,

this state of inner wakefulness becomes stabilized; the nervous system

gains the ability to maintain unbounded awareness even during the activ-

ity of daily life. The perfect orderliness and stability that charac-

terize consciousness in its least excited state begin to shine through

every thought and action. Mind and body become more integrated; inner

and outer conflicts cease; knowledge is given and gained without effort;

and intention flows unrestricted toward the desired goal. Throughout all

the changes of life, the stability and authority of the most silent level

of consciousness are maintained--one remains awake to oneself.

From the earliest days of the TM movement, it was predicted that the

increased orderliness, stability, intelligence and strength in the indi-

viduals practicing the TM technique would inevitably produce a similar

influence on the environment. Indeed, preliminary research indicates

lower crime, sickness and accident rates in areas where 1% of the popula-

tion practices the TM program. As more and more individuals begin the TM

technique and rise to enlightenment, it becomes possible to envision an

"Ideal Society," where each individual has use of his full potential and

therefore is contributing a maximum toward a progressive, harmonious life

for his family, community and society.

There is a standard seven-step program for learning the TM

WORLD PLAN EXECUTIVE COUNCIL   Page 6

Literature, Ethics, Recruiting, Relationships

BASIC BELIEFS (continued): techniques, including lectures, personal instruc-
    tion, and meetings. Follow-up meetings and courses are optional.

AUTHORITATIVE LITERATURE: There is no Bible or Holy Book as such. Factual
    information is provided in: Bloomfield, TM: Discovering Inner Energy
    and Overcoming Stress; Denniston and McWilliams, The TM Book; Forem,
    Transcendental Meditation, Maharishi Mahesh Yogi and the Science of Crea-
    tive Intelligence; and in Invitation to Create an Ideal Society, issued
    by the World Plan Executive Council, 1976.

ETHICAL PRACTICES: The TM program requires no specific faith, belief, accep-
    tance of a creed, changes in affiliations, or modification of diet, pos-
    ture or personal preferences. Goals of the World Plan for the Age of En-
    lightenment are: (1) to develop the full potential of the individual,
    (2) to improve governmental achievements, (3) to realize the highest
    ideal of education, (4) to eliminate the age-old problem of crime and all
    behavior that brings unhappiness to the family of man, (5) to maximize
    the intelligent use of the environment, (6) to bring fulfillment to the
    economic aspirations of individuals and society, and (7) to achieve the
    spiritual goals of mankind in this generation.

HOW DOES THE WORLD PLAN EXECUTIVE COUNCIL RECRUIT? Initially through recommen-
    dations of meditating family and friends. Currently most centers, in an
    effort to make the program more widely available to the public, advertise
    their introductory lectures as much as possible through local media.

RELATIONSHIPS WITH OTHER RELIGIONS OR GROUPS: Since the TM program is not a
    religion, it is compatible with all religions and faiths.

INTRODUCTION: ISLAMIC GROUPS

Islam, meaning to surrender or to submit (to Allah), was transmitted through the Prophet Muhammad who was born in the Arabian town of Mecca in A.D. 570. He started to preach Islam in the same town in A.D. 610. In 622 he emigrated to Medina, 280 miles north of Mecca, where Islam flourished and continued to grow. By 632, when the Prophet died, Islam had dominated all the Arabian peninsula. In a few more decades, it gained supremacy in the whole region of the Middle East.

It has been estimated that there are approximately 2,000,000 Muslims in the U.S. Muslims began to immigrate here, seeking a better living, about 1890 or 1900. Mostly they came from the Middle East and some came as seamen from Asia, first settling in port cities. The number of immigrants progressively increased after the First World War, bringing, in addition, Russian and other Muslim nationalities, and soon Muslim groups and societies began to spring up. Islam also has won local converts through zealous Americans who came into contact with Islam during the war. Islamic centers and mosques in the U.S. were established beginning in the early 1950's.

The religion of Islam is based on the Glorious Qur'an, or Koran, the sacred Book of Islam. In addition, the words and practices of the Prophet Muhammand, known as HADITH, serve as a second source, which unfolds and inter- prets the Qur'anic text.

The emphasis of Islamic teachings is summed up in the Koran Sura (Chapter) 4:135: "Believe in God and His apostle and the Book which he has sent down formerly. He who disbelieves in God and His angels, His Book and His apostles and the last day, has strayed far (from the Truth)." Muslims believe in the unity of God, in the Angels, in all the Messengers of God (including Adam,

Noah, Abraham, Moses, Jesus, and Muhammad); in the Sacred Books, including

the Torah, the Gospels, the Psalms, and the Koran), and in the Day of Judg-

ment. All followers of Muhammad observe the five basic duties of worship,

namely: (1) to proclaim the Shahadah (confession of the faith); (2) to per-

form the mandatory five daily prayers on time; (3) to fast the month of

Ramadan, the ninth in the lunar calendar, from dawn to sunset; (4) to pay (to

the poor) Zakat (taxes or religious *tithes* on certain properties), including

the zakat due at the end of Ramadan; and (5) to perform pilgrimage in Mecca,

at least once in a lifetime.

In general, Islam has no centralized authorities, no group of "priests."

The individual's bond with God is considered to be direct with no intermediary.

There are "religious" scholars or teachers who, in view of their academic attain

ment or superior understanding, can answer inquiries, often serve in leadership

roles, and are regarded as authorities on theological questions. There are

also Islamic organizations in America of which the Council of Imams may be re-

garded as the highest body on Islamic theology and canon law.

During the early 1900's, Muslim groups in the U.S. consisted largely of

immigrants and local converts, predominantly among non-blacks. However, as

early as 1913, Timothy Drew Ali, "Prophet of Islam," had emerged in Newark,

New Jersey. He believed that only Islam could unite the black people, whose

true heritage was Moorish. In 1921, Dr. Mufti Muhammad Sadiz, a member of the

Ahmadiyya Muslims arrived in Chicago and began to gather converts. His success,

primarily among black people, was due to an emphasis on the basic message of

human equality.

In the 1930's, Islam also began to find a receptive audience among black

people in the northern urban centers. While many of the slaves brought to

America were Muslims, the movement in the years of the Great Depression was
a new phenomenon. Among the followers of Black Nationalist Marcus Garvey,
was an Egyptian Blackman Duse Mohammed Ali, and Garvey lauded the black
people of ancient Egypt and the medieval Moorish empires in his newspaper,
The Negro World. Contact between American blacks and Islam increased as a
result of World War I.

At present, over 15 Islamic groups exist in the United States. A focal
point for orthodox Islam is the Islamic Center in Washington, D.C.

The World Community of Islam in the West and the Hanafi Muslim Movement
are two of the larger Islamic groups drawing primarily on the black community
for members. Other similar groups include the Moorish Science Temple (of
Noble Drew Ali), the Ahmadiyya Muslim Movement, and the Nubian Islamic Hebrew
Mission.

In general, Muslims consider Islam to be a unified religion. Variations
in cultural or ethnic heritage or religious tradition have resulted in a
number of groupings, however. Among these are groups which have chosen to
identify with the early ascetic and mystical movement known as Sufism.

The Sufi Order is the largest of some 10 Sufi groups, most of which have
arisen in the 20th century. The Habibiyya-Shadhiliyya Order is a classic
dervish group. Sufism Reoriented organizes the followers of modern Sufi
Master Meher Baba. Other groups are built around Sufi teachers G.I. Gurjieff
Pak Sabuh. E.J. Gold. and Guru Bawa.

THE HANAFI MUSLIM MOVEMENT 7700 - 16th Street, N.W. Washington, D.C. 20012	Hamaas Abdul Khaalis, Chief Imam

HISTORICAL ROOTS: The Hanafi Muslim Movement participates in the wider Community of Islam that began with the Prophet Muhammad who was born in the city of Mecca in 570 AD. In the early 1930s, Islam began to be accepted among the black people of America.

CURRENT WORLD LEADER: Hamaas Abdul Khaalis, Chief Imam.

ORIGINS IN THE U.S.: The Hanafi movement began among members of the Nation of Islam (now the World Community of Islam in the West). Hamaas Abdul Khaalis embraced the Black Muslim faith in 1950, and became the National Secretary of the Nation of Islam in 1956. His sincere conviction that the Nation of Islam was not following the true way of the Musselman (Muslim), and his commitment to the traditional Sunni way led to his departure from the Nation of Islam in 1958. In 1968, Khaalis established the Hanafi Madh-Hab Center in New York, then moved the Hanafi headquarters to Washington, D.C., in 1972.

NUMBER OF ADHERENTS IN THE U.S.: Unknown. Membership centers around Mosques in New York, Washington, Chicago, and Los Angeles.

ORGANIZATIONAL STRUCTURE: Authority for the Hanafi Muslims is vested in the Chief Imam. Each mosque is headed by an Imam appointed by Khaalis.

LEADERSHIP AND ROLE OF IMAMS: Imams are the chief religious scholars in the Muslim faith. They assume leadership responsibility for all religious activities, deliver sermons, lead in prayers, render counsel, officiate at conversions and marriages, and direct the mosque activities.

WHO MAY CONDUCT WORSHIP SERVICES? Any Hanafi may conduct services. The deeper his knowledge, the more he is entitled to do so.

THE HANAFI MUSLIM MOVEMENT   Page 2

Worship, Requirements

IS GROUP WORSHIP REQUIRED? Yes, especially on Friday. Noon prayer is also
     required, and observance of each of the five daily prayers is expected.

WORSHIP REQUIREMENTS: Hanafis observe the five basic duties of worship (see
     "Basic Teachings or Beliefs"). The body must be washed and neatly
     dressed for prayer.

MINIMUM EQUIPMENT FOR WORSHIP: The Holy Qur'an (Koran) and other literature
     (Hadith) which reveals the teachings of Prophet Muhammad, and a prayer
     rug or mat.

FACILITIES FOR WORSHIP: A mosque or other facility providing the necessary
     area for use of prayer rugs and observance of the worship requirements
     (see "Basic Teachings or Beliefs").

OTHER SPECIFIC RELIGIOUS REQUIREMENTS OTHER THAN WORSHIP: During the month of
     Ramadan, the meal schedule must be adjusted so that no food is taken from
     sunrise to sunset. At the end of the month, a small charity must be given
     to the poor (alms) (see also "Basic Teachings or Beliefs").

DIETARY LAWS OR RESTRICTIONS: Pork and its derivatives, intoxicating liquors
     and harmful drugs are prohibited.

SPECIAL RELIGIOUS HOLIDAYS: Besides the regular Friday worship with prayer,
     the Hanafis keep the Fast of Ramadan. During this period (which varies
     annually as it is figured on the lunar calendar) no food is eaten between
     sunrise and sunset. Diet and meals are regulated accordingly.

FUNERAL AND BURIAL REQUIREMENTS: The body must be washed, wrapped, and
     shrouded. Funeral prayer service accompanies burial.

AUTOPSY: Not allowed unless required by law.

CREMATION: Not allowed. Body must be returned to earth in its original form
    and shape.

MEDICAL TREATMENT: Generally no restrictions except that no intoxicants may
    be taken.

UNIFORM APPEARANCE REQUIREMENTS: Women should be covered completely, exposing
    their body only below the ankles and elbows. Heads must be covered. The
    body must always be cleanly covered, especially during prayer.

POSITION ON SERVICE IN THE ARMED FORCES: Hanafis see it as necessary for pur-
    poses of defense, especially when the lives, freedom or personal property
    of Muslims are threatened.

IS A MINISTER OR IMAM REQUIRED AT TIME OF DEATH? The presence is desirable but
    not necessarily required.

ANY OTHER PRACTICES OR TEACHINGS WHICH MAY CONFLICT WITH MILITARY DIRECTIVES
    OR PRACTICE: None, except the prohibition against eating pork and the
    required fast of Ramadan. In general, Hanafis believe in obedience to the
    laws and authority of the country unless they conflict with Muslim law.
    Muslim law then would take priority.

BASIC TEACHINGS OR BELIEFS: The basic Muslim teachings form the basis for
    Hanafi beliefs. These include belief in: (1) Allah, the Supreme God, and
    His Will and Teachings as Revealed to His Prophet Muhammad; (2) studying
    the Holy Qur'an (Koran) and respecting it as the one most authoritative
    source of the teachings of Islam; and (3) observing the moral and legal
    codes of Islam.

THE HANAFI MUSLIM MOVEMENT	Page 4

Basic Beliefs, Literature, Ethics, Recruiting, Relationships

BASIC BELIEFS (continued): Hanafis believe in observing the basic duties of Islamic worship, including (1) proclaim the Shahadah (confession of Faith); (2) mandatory prayer five times daily; (3) month of fasting (Ramadan 9th in the lunar calendar); (4) Zakat (taxes and *tithes* for the poor); and (5) performance of a pilgrimage to Mecca at least once in a lifetime.

CREEDAL STATEMENTS AND/OR AUTHORITATIVE LITERATURE: The Holy Qur'an (Koran) and the Hadith (the words and practices of the Prophet Muhammad) are considered authoritative. Writings of Hamaas Abdul Khaalis are sometimes used to describe the faith, but are not "authoritative."

ETHICAL PRACTICES: Hanafis encourage good conduct, chastity, and honest dealing. The members also stress equality and justice to all, and they take seriously the law -- "An eye for an eye and a tooth for a tooth."

HOW DO THE HANAFI MUSLIMS RECRUIT MEMBERS? By word of mouth and passing out literature. There is no real recruitment program.

RELATIONSHIP WITH OTHER RELIGIONS: Cordial with most religions. Hanafis respect Christians, Hindus, Buddhists, etc., but reject those beliefs and practices which are contrary to the teachings of Islam. While Hanafis have generally rejected the racial nature of much of the early Black Muslim movement, they believe strongly in defending their faith against "the enemies of Islam."

THE SUFI ORDER   Sikander Coppleman
P.O. Box 396
New Lebanon, New York 12125

HISTORICAL ROOTS: The Sufi Order is a universal esoteric school which has

grown through the centuries out of a meeting and blending of several

religious traditions. Sufism can truly be traced to mystical tenden-

cies within the first generation of Islam, the religious heritage in

which it has grown, but can also be traced to the teachings of the

Zoroastrian Magi communicated to the early esotericists of Islam and to

the great Mystic Suhrawardi and his philosophy of Illumination.

Sufism developed mainly in Persia and Arabia where it found an

alliance with the Hellenic philosophy of Avicenna. The contact with the

Syrian monks (Christians) accounts for the origin of the term Sufi from

"suf" wool, the dress of the hermits. Through the years, various mystic

traditions--Buddhism, Vedanta, and Spanish mysticism--added their rich-

ness to Sufism.

In India, Vedanta and Sufism came together in the work of Khwaja

Muinuddin Chishti, founder of the Order that bears his name. The Chishti

Order has since the thirteenth century seen Sufism's mission to cohere

religions finally into unity. The Sufi Order represents a transplanting

of the Chishti Order to the West.

CURRENT WORLD LEADER: Present head of the Sufi Order is Pir Vilayat Kan, son

of the founder of the Order, Hazrat Inayat Khan.

ORIGINS IN THE UNITED STATES: The Sufi Order was founded by Hazrat Pir-O-

Murshid Inayat Khan (1882-1927), a musician known for his accomplishments

in classical Indian music, and a mystic. He was nominated by Hazrat Abu

Hashim Madani, successor in line to Khwaja Muinuddin Chishti, as his

THE SUFI ORDER	Page 2
Origins, Organization, Leadership, Worship	

ORIGINS (continued): successor and was assigned the task of bringing Sufism to the West. He first traveled to the United States and to Europe in 1910, gathering disciples and forming centers. He resided near Paris and continued to teach and lead the order until his death. His son succeeded him and continues to guide the work.

NUMBER OF ADHERENTS IN THE UNITED STATES: Approximately 5,000.

ORGANIZATIONAL STRUCTURE: The Sufi Order is built around a number of local centers, each headed by a leader appointed by Pir Vilayat Khan, the head of the Order. The center at New Lebanon, recently purchased from the Shakers, also functions as the headquarters in the United States. From there the monthly The Message is produced.

LEADERSHIP AND ROLE OF MINISTERS: Local leaders coordinate the activities of the local center, holding meetings to train initiates and conducting universal worship services. Most leaders are cherags, or ministers, but not all cherags are local leaders.

WHO MAY CONDUCT WORSHIP SERVICES? Any cherag (minister) of the Order.

IS GROUP WORSHIP REQUIRED? No.

WORSHIP REQUIREMENTS: None, though most Sufis practice meditation regularly. However, each center offers a weekly Universal Worship Service as well as regular classes in meditation, spiritual dance, and Sufism. The spiritual dance, popularly known as "dervish" dancing is an earmark of Sufism.

MINIMUM EQUIPMENT FOR WORSHIP: Candles.

FACILITIES FOR WORSHIP: None.

THE SUFI ORDER   Page 3

Requirements, Position on Service, Basic Beliefs

OTHER SPECIFIC RELIGIOUS REQUIREMENTS OTHER THAN WORSHIP: Members meet

    regularly (at least once a month) with a local leader or initiator.

    Private meditation practice is required daily.

DIETARY LAWS OF RESTRICTIONS: None.

SPECIAL RELIGIOUS HOLIDAYS: Because of the universal nature of the Sufi per-

    spective, all holidays of all major faiths tend to be celebrated, but

    within the Order, the anniversary of the death of the founder, February

    5, is especially noted.

FUNERAL AND BURIAL REQUIREMENTS: None.

AUTOPSY: No restrictions.

CREMATIONS: No restrictions.

MEDICAL TREATMENT: No restrictions.

UNIFORM APPEARANCE REQUIREMENTS: No restrictions.

POSITION ON SERVICE IN THE ARMED FORCES: None.

IS A MINISTER (CHERAG) REQUIRED AT TIME OF DEATH? No.

ANY OTHER PRACTICES OR TEACHINGS WHICH MAY CONFLICT WITH MILITARY DIRECTIVES

    OR PRACTICE: None.

BASIC TEACHINGS OR BELIEFS: The object of the Sufi Order is: (1) to realize

    the knowledge of unity, the religion of love and wisdom, so that the bias

    of faiths and beliefs may of itself fall away, the human heart may over-

    flow with love, and all hatred caused by distinctions and differences may

    be rooted out. (2) To discover the light and power latent in man, the

    secret of all religion, the power of mysticism, and the essence of

    philosophy, without interfering with customs or belief. (3) To help

BASIC BELIEFS (continued): bring the world's two opposite poles, East and
West, closer together by the interchange of thought and ideals, that the
Universal Brotherhood may form of itself, and man may see with man be-
yond the narrow national and racial boundaries.

To that end, the Sufi Order teaches: "(1) There is One God, the
Eternal, the Only Being; none else exists save He. (2) There is one
Master, the Guiding Spirit of all Souls, who constantly leads his followers toward the light. (3) There is one Holy Book, the sacred manu-
script of nature, the only scripture which can enlighten the reader.
(4) There is one Religion, the unswerving progress in the right direction toward the ideal, which fulfills the life's purpose of every soul.
(5) There is one Law, the law of reciprocity, which can be observed by
a selfless conscience together with a sense of awakened justice. (6)
There is one Brotherhood, the human brotherhood, which unites the children of earth indiscriminately in the Fatherhood of God. (7) There is
one Moral Principle, the love which springs forth from self-denial, and
blooms in deeds of beneficence. (8) There is one Object of Praise, the
beauty which uplifts the heart of its worshiper through all aspects from
the seen to the unseen. (9) There is one Truth, the true knowledge of
our being within and without, which is the essence of all wisdom. (10)
There is one Path, the annihilation of the false ego in the real, which
raises the mortal to immortality and in which resides all perfection."
CREEDAL STATEMENTS AND/OR AUTHORITATIVE LITERATURE: The Sufi Order does not
have a Bible as such, but uses the inspiration that shines through all

THE SUFI ORDER   Page 5

Literature, Ethics, Recruiting, Relationships

LITERATURE (continued): sacred writings. The teachings of the founder are
    found in his multi-volume collected works, the Sufi Message.

ETHICAL PRACTICES: (See "Basic Beliefs," especially numbers 5 to 7.)

HOW DOES THE SUFI ORDER RECRUIT MEMBERS? The Sufi Order holds public pro-
    grams regularly around the country as well as meditation camps to which
    prospective members and others may come. The major growth has taken
    place by word-of-mouth sharing of the Sufi experience.

RELATIONSHIPS WITH OTHER RELIGIONS: Implicit in Sufism is an openness and
    search for unity with the religions of the world. Sufism seeks to
    illuminate each religions' essence and unity.

THE WORLD COMMUNITY OF ISLAM IN THE WEST Masjid Honorable Elijah Muhammad 7351 S. Stony Island Chicago, Illinois 60649	Wallace D. Muhammad, Chief Eman AKA: Black Muslims

HISTORICAL ROOTS: The World Community of Islam in the West began as the
Black Muslim Movement, or the Nation of Islam, in the early 1930's. A
peddler, with the use of a Qur'an (book composed of writings accepted by
the Muslims as revelations), began teaching the black ghetto of Detroit
the origins of blacks, nutritional guides, and what constituted the
"true" religion of the black man. His teachings became bitter denounce-
ments against the white race. This peddler, Farad Mohammad (one of
several names), disappeared in 1934 and was succeeded by his most trusted
student and follower, Elijah Poole. Poole, later renamed Elijah Muhammed, continued in the footsteps of the mysterious peddler by denouncing
Christianity and the white race.

CURRENT WORLD LEADER: The Chief Eman (spiritual leader), Wallace D. Muhammad,
son of Elijah Muhammad.

ORIGINS IN THE U.S.: Another follower, Abdul Muhammad, withdrew and established a temple in Detroit. Competition between Elijah Muhammad and
Abdul Muhammad became so fierce that Elijah Muhammad relocated and
established another temple in Chicago. From 1934 to his death, 1975,
Elijah Muhammad emerged as the undisputed leader of the Nation of Islam.
He made a science of black nationalism, requesting black separation from
white, "blue-eye" devils (white people). In 1959, the movement received an extra boost with the conversion of Malcolm X. Malcolm emerged
as a dynamic spokesman for Muhammad. In 1965, the time of Malcolm's
death, the movement consisted of 70 temples throughout the United States.

THE WORLD COMMUNITY OF ISLAM IN THE WEST	Page 2
Origins, Organization, Leadership	

ORIGINS (continued): Wallace Muhammad still directs the movement from its
national headquarters in Chicago, and has made drastic changes in the
movement, in an effort to move closer in belief and practice, to orthodox Islam. Whites are no longer attacked (they are encouraged to join)
and Christianity is no longer attacked to the extent that it once was.
The movement was influenced from its beginning by black nationalist
movements, i.e., Moorish Science Temple and the Marcus Garvey Movement.

NUMBER OF ADHERENTS: About 150,000.

ORGANIZATIONAL STRUCTURE: Wallace D. Muhammad is the Chief Iman (spiritual
leader and chief minister of the movement), chosen and approved as the
new leader of the movement after the death of his father, Elijah Muhammad. The movement also consists of Muslim ministers who, in view of
their expertise, are regarded as authorities on theological questions.
Many of these ministers assist the Chief Minister, Wallace Muhammad, and
are spokesmen or leaders in 65-70 temples throughout the U.S. Also, a
Iman Consultation Board functions as an authority on the beliefs,
rituals, and practices of the World Community, under the directorship
of Sheikh James Abdul Aziz Shabazz.

LEADERSHIP AND THE ROLE OF THE MINISTERS: There is no "priesthood" or *ordin-
dination."* Muslim ministers are teachers who exemplify the greatest
degree of knowledge, assume religious responsibilities, deliver mes-
sages from the Holy Koran, lead in prayers, render counsel, officiate
at conversions and marriages, and are chosen and approved by the great
body of the movement.

Worship, Requirements

WHO MAY CONDUCT WORSHIP SERVICES? Any muslim, however, services are usually

conducted by ministers of the various Temples or Mosques. The Chief

Iman, Chief minister, and spiritual leader, may also conduct services.

Designated ministers in every Temple, who possess deep knowledge, lead

in prayers on Fridays (noon prayer) and Sundays.

IS GROUP WORSHIP REQUIRED? Yes, for noon prayers on Fridays. Group worship

is highly recommended for each of the five daily prayers. Members are

also encouraged to attend and support Sunday services.

WORSHIP REQUIREMENTS: The body must be cleaned (face, mouth, nostrils,

arms, etc.), and so must the member's clothing and the place of worship.

MINIMUM EQUIPMENT FOR WORSHIP: Each member must have a prayer mat or rug

for prayer on Fridays and Sundays. A podium or platform is also

desireable for the prayer leader and the minister who gives the message.

FACILITIES FOR WORSHIP: Temple or Mosque.

OTHER SPECIFIC RELIGIOUS REQUIREMENTS OTHER THAN WORSHIP: During the Month

of Ramadan, which is observed by all Muslims, meal schedules are

adjusted. Muslims are required to abstain from food between dawn and

dusk. At the end of the Month of Ramadan, a prayer celebration takes

place along with the practice of almsgiving (contributing to the poor

and needy). Every Muslim is encouraged to take a trip to Mecca during

his lifetime, a practice that apparently was not encouraged while the

movement was known as the Black Muslim Movement.

THE WORLD COMMUNITY OF ISLAM IN THE WEST	Page 4

Requirements

DIETARY LAWS OR RESTRICTIONS: Pork and its derivatives are prohibited.

Alcoholic beverages and drug abuse are forbidden.

SPECIAL RELIGIOUS HOLIDAYS: The World Community celebrates the birthday of

the Prophet Muhammad, born in Mecca in A.D. 570. Every Friday is a

special day in which all Muslims are obligated to participate in the

noon prayers (Juma prayers). The 30 days of Ramadan, which marks the

period of Muslim fasting are celebrated. The climax of the fast of

Ramadan is also marked by prayer and celebration. Since the Muslim

calendar is eleven days less every year, these holidays do not represent

permanent dates on the Gregorian calendar.

FUNERAL AND BURIAL REQUIREMENTS: At the time of death, members pray for

the soul of the deceased. The body is washed, two pieces of cotton

placed in the mouth, one in each ear, one in the anus. The eyes and

sexual organs are covered. The body is then wrapped in a cotton sheet

and a simple prayer is said for the soul of the deceased member.

IS A MINISTER REQUIRED AT TIME OF DEATH? Presence of any Muslim is desired.

AUTOPSY: Allowed if necessary and/or required by law.

CREMATION: Not allow. The body should return to earth in natural form.

MEDICAL TREATMENT: No restrictions.

UNIFORM OR APPEARANCE REQUIREMENTS: Men are forbidden to wear tight clothes

which show the print of the body. Women should also be decently dressed;

the body should be completely clothed, showing only the face, hands, and

below the ankles.

Position on Service, Basic Beliefs, Ethics

POSITION ON SERVICE IN THE ARMED FORCES: Members of the World Community will

go to war to defend the Muslim people, or the country in which Muslim

people reside.

OTHER PRACTICES OR TEACHINGS WHICH MAY CONFLICT WITH MILITARY DIRECTIVES

OR PRACTICE: None other than worship requirements.

CREEDAL STATEMENTS AND/OR AUTHORITATIVE LITERATURE: The religion of the

World Community is based on the Holy Koran (Qur'an), the Sacred Book

of Islam. The articles and essays written by the Chief Minister and

other ministers and administrators in the World Community's newspaper,

Bilalian News, are also considered authoritative.

BASIC TEACHINGS AND BELIEFS: Muslims are taught to hold fast the creed of

Islam, which encourages the fervent belief in Allah as the One true

and Supreme God, and belief in Muhammad as his Holy Prophet and Servant.

The movement teaches complete obedience and submission to Allah, and

respect for His divine Prophet, Muhammad. It also teaches - All the

Prophets are authentic and were sent from God - Moses, Abraham, Jesus,

Buddha, Muhammad, etc. The divine message of Allah and the Holy

Prophet Muhammad is disclosed. The basic duties of worship should be

observed; namely, to perform the five daily prayers, to fast the Month

of Ramadan, pay or give alms to the poor and take a trip to Mecca. It

also stresses the brotherhood of all men as part of its basic teachings.

ETHICAL PRACTICES: The World Community emphasizes proper ethical practices

such as cleanliness, good conduct, chastity, charity, honesty, courtesy,

THE WORLD COMMUNITY OF ISLAM IN THE WEST	Page 6

Ethics, Recruiting, Relationships

ETHICAL PRACTICES (continued): proper appearance, etc. It also stresses

brotherhood, equality, justice, and love.

HOW DOES THE GROUP RECRUIT MEMBERS? Conversion takes place, generally, on

a voluntary basis. The members recruit by word of mouth and by passing

out flyers and membership cards to visitors of the temples.

RELATIONSHIP TO OTHER RELIGIONS: The members agree that there is authentic-

ity in all religions and express the need for religious heads to come

together in an effort for human survival. For this reason, and because

all religions and prophets are respected, tolerance of other religions

is encouraged. Despite its policy of tolerance, the World Community's

relationships with other Muslim groups has not always been strong. A

recent visit to the Mideast by Wallace Muhammed has strengthened ties

with most of the Muslim world, but relationships with such groups as

the Hanafi Muslims in the U.S. are precarious. The World Community

does believe that Muslims are Muslims, without the need for distinc-

tions. Unlike many other Muslims groups, however, the World Community

still maintains strict security.

INTRODUCTION: JAPANESE HERITAGE GROUPS

Although members of "Japanese Heritage" groups are by no means limited to persons of Japanese descent, the origins of these religions in the United States can generally be traced to the arrival of the first Japanese immigrants. In general, this immigration began in 1868, when 148 contract laborers arrived in Hawaii, the first of thousands of Japanese who were to work on the Hawaiian plantations. Within a few years, Japamese immigrants began to arrive on the West Coast, particularly in California. Japanese Americans now number more than 500,000, 85 percent of whom still reside in Hawaii and on the West Coast.

The immigrants brought their religions--Shinto and Buddhism--with them. In 1889 Soryu Kagaki of the Honpa Honwangi, the largest of the Buddhist groups, arrived in Honolulu and began work among the plantation workers. In April of that year a temple was constructed in Hilo. In the remaining years of the century, priests of other groups--Jodo-shu, Higashi Hongwangi and Soto Zen-- began their efforts.

Prior to the sixth century A.D., the predominant religion of Japan was the Shinto faith. Indigenous to Japan, Shinto consists chiefly in the reverence of the spirits of natural forces, emperors, and heroes.

Buddhism entered Japan in the sixth century A.D. from Korea. In 710, at the time of the building of the new capitol at Nara, the emperor became Buddhist and made Buddhism the state religion. Several varieties of Buddhism were introduced, but the next centuries saw the emergence of the more popular forms. The popularity of Buddhism in the country depended directly upon the favor of the various emperors.

The twelfth century saw the arrival of Honen and Shinran from China. They introduced what became the most popular form of Buddhism, the Pure Land. Pure Land Buddhism teaches devotion to Amida Buddha. Sincere invocation of this bodhisattva (saint) gives entrance into the Pure Land (heaven).

The following century saw the appearance of Nichiren, a Buddhist reformer whose efforts led to the founding of the Nichiren-shu. Nichiren was attached to the Lotus Sutra, a collection of Buddha's teaching, which he believed contained the primitive true Buddhism that could unite the various groups.

The last major Buddhist group to enter Japan was the Zen school which came from China. Combining the strong meditative practices of Chinese Taoism with Buddhist tradition, Tao-sheng (360-434) the founder, added an emphasis on the possibility of instantaneous enlightenment.

The modern history of Japanese religion began with the revival of "pure" Shinto whose exponents wished to stop the assimilation of Shinto into Buddhism. Their efforts led to the establishment of the National Learning School to spread the nationalist-oriented traditions. A major outcome of the revived Shinto was the restoration of Imperial authority under Emperor Meiji. Shinto grew in power steadily until World War II.

The nineteenth and twentieth centuries saw the greatest divergence develop in Japanese religion. Christianity entered and established a strong mission. The older forms of Buddhism and Shinto became divided. New religions drawing on a variety of sources, including private revelations, were begun. Collectively, these new indigenous groups have been termed the "New Religions." Many of these groups were suppressed under the Shinto revival.

The declaration of religious freedom under the Allied occupation of Japan after World War II freed the "New Religions" to expand. Some--such

as Rissho Kosei Kai, Tenrikyo, and Konko Kyo--have become international faiths
with strong followings in the United States.

There are no less than forty groups of Japanese origin functioning in
the United States. Most are Buddhist, but Shinto and the New Religions are
well represented. The Buddhist groups share allegiance to Siddhartha Guatama,
the Buddha, the Enlightened One. In 529 B.C., he abandoned his princely life
and family to wander in search of the meaning of life. His search ended in
523 B.C.; while in meditation and contemplation, he found enlightenment.
At that point, he became the Buddha.

Buddhist teachings were collected into the Tripitaka, the Three Baskets,
which includes the Vinaya, the Sutras, and the Abhidharma. The Vinaya contains the story of Buddha's life and the rules for the monks. The Sutras
contain Buddha's teachings along with those of his close disciples. The
Abhidharma contains Buddha's discourses.

The Buddhist Churches of America, the largest Buddhist group in America,
is the American form of the Honpa Hongwangi Pure Land Buddhism. Other Pure
Land groups in the United States are the Higashi Hongwangi Buddhist Church
and the Jodo Mission.

The Nichiren Shoshu or Soka Gakkai is the largest of several Nichiren
groups in America. Other bodies include the older Nichiren Mission and the
Rissho Kosei Kai.

The Church of Perfect Liberty is one of the largest of the New Religions
and shows some of their diverse and eclectic nature.

BUDDHIST CHURCHES OF AMERICA 1710 Octavia Street San Francisco, California 94109	Rev. Kenryu T. Tsuji Presiding Bishop AKA: BCA; Shin Buddhism, Jodo Shinshu Denom.

HISTORICAL ROOTS: The Founder of Buddhism was Gautama, the Buddha, born in 566 B.C., son of a king in Kapilavastu, which is present day Nepal. The Shin sect of Buddhism gradually grew from the teachings of Shinran Shonin (1173-1262 A.D.) who had left the monastery, married and preached Buddhism according to his own Buddhistic experience.

CURRENT WORLD LEADER ("PATRIARCH"): Koshin Otani, Twenty-fourth Descendant of Shinran Shonin, in Japan.

ORIGINS IN THE U.S.: On July 6, 1898, Rev. Eryu Honda and Rev. Ejun Miyamoto arrived in the U.S. on a goodwill visit. They came to view the living condition of Japanese immigrants and to explore the possibility of extending the teachings in the U.S. As a result of this visit, Rev. S. Sonoda and Rev. Kakuryo Nishijima were sent to the U.S. as the first official missionaries, arriving in San Francisco on September 1, 1899. Temples were erected wherever Japanese immigrants had settled, to meet the needs of the Japanese population. Currently there are 60 independent temples and 40 branches in the Mainland U.S., and an independent sister organization, the Hongwanji Mission of Hawaii, organized in the Hawaiian Islands.

NUMBER OF ADHERENTS IN THE U.S.: Approximately 60,000 to 100,000.

ORGANIZATIONAL STRUCTURE: At the national headquarters, administrative duties are conducted by the Office of the Bishop, the Executive Secretary and Secretarial Staff. Churches and branches are divided geographically into eight districts: Southern: essentially Arizona and Southern California; Central: essentially Central California (Fresno, Bakersfield); Coast:

Organization, Leadership

ORGANIZATIONAL STRUCTURE (continued): California coast, Mountain View/San Jose

to Monterey; Bay: San Francisco Area, (Palo Alto to Sebastopol); Northern

California (Sacramento to Marysville); Northwest: Washington, Oregon, and

Idaho; Mountain: the Rocky Mountain Area (Utah, Colorado, etc.); Eastern:

from the Twin Cities (Minnesota) to New York. Each district is repre-

sented by a Minister-Director selected by ministers of the respective

districts, and by three district-representatives selected by the District

Council.

Affiliated organizations are maintained by each church to meet

spiritual, social and educational needs of all age group members. Prin-

cipal organizations: The Buddhist Women's Association, Adult Buddhist

Association, Young Buddhist Association and Sunday School Teachers

Association, all organized into large leagues and federations. One

representative from each league or federation represents each at the BCA

Board of Directors meetings.

Educational centers in the U.S. are the Institute of Buddhist

Studies, 2717 Haste Street, Berkeley, California 94704, and the American

Buddhist Academy, 332 Riverside Drive, New York, New York 10025.

Lectures, pre-ministerial training, in-service ministerial seminars, lay

leader training and other educational programs are conducted at the

centers, which may be contacted directly for information.

LEADERSHIP AND ROLE OF MINISTERS: The Board of Directors is composed of the

BUDDHIST CHURCHES OF AMERICA	Page 3

Worship, Requirements

LEADERSHIP (Continued) Presiding Bishop (Rev. Kenryu T. Tsuji), the

Honorary Chairman, the Chairman of the Ministerial Association, Pres-

ident and President-elect, 9 Directors-at-large elected at the annual

National Council meeting, 24 district representatives, 8 Minister-

directors, 4 representatives of affiliated organizations, and one im-

mediate past president of the BCA Board of Directors. The Board of

Directors president presides over all meetings of the Board of Di-

rectors and the National Council.

Over 80 ministers actively serving the spiritual needs of the

Buddhists of Jodo Shinshu faith constitute the BCA Ministerial Asso-

ciation. The Chairman of the Ministerial Association presides over the

affairs of the Ministerial Association and represents the ministers at

the BCA Board of Directors Meetings.

WHO MAY CONDUCT WORSHIP SERVICES? Any member, individually or in groups.

IS GROUP WORSHIP REQUIRED? No.

WORSHIP REQUIREMENTS: Although there are no specific requirements, worship-

ers recite the name, Namu Amida Butsu, literally meaning "I place my

faith in Amida Buddha" (see also "Basic Teachings and Beliefs").

MINIMUM EQUIPMENT FOR WORSHIP: Statue or scroll of Amida Buddha or Scroll

of the Sacred Name, Namu Amida Butsu, desirable but not absolutely

necessary.

FACILITIES FOR WORSHIP: Table for scroll or statue, incense and incense

burner, flower and flower vase, and candle and single candle stand

if available.

OTHER SPECIFIC RELIGIOUS REQUIREMENTS OTHER THAN WORSHIP: None.

BUDDHIST CHURCHES OF AMERICA	Page 4

Requirements, Holidays, Position on Service

DIETARY LAWS OR RESTRICTIONS: None, although individuals, depending upon their individual temperaments, may follow their own diet, e.g., vegetarian, etc.

SPECIAL RELIGIOUS HOLIDAYS: There are 11 days observed by BCA as special for focusing on Buddhist heritage and practice. These are: January 1 (Shusho E), a day of dedication; January 16 (Ho-on-ko), gratitude in memory of Shinran Shonin: February 15 (Nehan E), observe Sakyamuni's passing into Nirvana; March 21 (Higan E), meditate on the harmony of nature; April 8 (Hanamatsuri), commemorate the birth of Gautama Buddha; May 21 (Shuso Gotan E), Shinran Shonin Day; July 15 (Bon), the "Gathering of Joy" rejoicing in enlightenment; September 1 (Beikoku Bukkyo Kaikyo Kinenbi), BCA Founding Day; September 23 (Higan E), recalling the Six Perfections; December 8 (Jodo E), Gautama's Enlightenment under the Bodhi Tree; December 13 (Joya E), Meditation on blessings and gratitude.

FUNERAL AND BURIAL REQUIREMENTS: Individual or family preferences honored.

AUTOPSY: Individual or family preferences honored.

CREMATION: Individual or family preferences honored.

MEDICAL TREATMENT: Individual or family preferences honored.

UNIFORM OR APPEARANCE REQUIREMENTS: None. Members encouraged to carry Nenju (Buddhist rosary) at all times.

POSITION ON SERVICE IN THE ARMED FORCES: Essentially non-violent, but individual preference is honored.

IS A MINISTER REQUIRED AT TIME OF DEATH? Not necessarily, but, if available, minister usually conducts bedside service at death.

ANY OTHER PRACTICES OR TEACHINGS WHICH MAY CONFLICT WITH MILITARY DIRECTIVES

OR PRACTICES? None. Buddhism is a religion with enlightenment as

its goals. Any experience, including the military, can and may lead

the way to enlightenment. However, Buddhism holds non-violence as the

highest ideal.

BASIC TEACHINGS AND BELIEFS: (See also "Worship Requirements.") Amida

Buddha is the symbolic Buddha of infinite Light and Life. Buddhism

is the way of developing the fullest potential in all human beings.

Some forms of Buddhism are not based on the spirit of Wisdom

and Compassion and their emphasis is on the historical Buddha. Jodo

Shinshu (see "Leadership and Role of Ministers") also presumes these

other forms of Buddhism to be valid. The power of sacred universal

salvation consummated by Amida is embodied in the sacred Name, Namu

Amida Butsu, which is easy to remember and recite. Amida Buddha

communicates with us through his Name, which has three aspects. Its

substance is the absolute power to save all sentient (aware) beings.

Its form is two-fold: it is Amida Buddha's voice calling to us and

our vocal response to his call. Its meaning is the actualization of

salvation and complete assurance of our Enlightenment. Wherever

there is "Namu Amida Butsu" there is Amida Buddha, and wherever there

is Amida Buddha there is "Namu Amida Butsu."

CREEDAL STATEMENTS AND/OR AUTHORITATIVE LITERATURE: From the voluminous

Buddhist Tripitaka, Shinran Shonin selected three sutras that bring

BUDDHIST CHURCHES OF AMERICA	Page 6
Basic Beliefs, Ethics, Recruiting, Relationships	

LITERATURE (continued): one directly to the heart of Amida Buddha. They are (1) The Large Sutra on the Eternal Life, in which *Sakyamuni* tells the Sangha about Amida Buddha; (2) the Meditation Sutra on the Eternal Buddha, showing the actual case of a woman who finds salvation through Amida Buddha; and (3) The Smaller Sutra on Amida Buddha, describing the beauty of the Pure Land and extolling the virtures of Amida Buddha.

ETHICAL PRACTICES: No specific set of ethical practices are set forth in Jodo Shinshu except for members to live a life of gratitude; gratitude is the way faith is expressed. Our life gives this faith the opportunity of expression.

HOW DOES THE BCA RECRUIT MEMBERS? Buddhism is a soft-sell kind of religion. If a person considers himself a Buddhist, he is a Buddhist. In its 2500 year history, Buddhism has not been involved in religious wars to convert people of other religions. Shin Buddhist missionaries seek people who have similar views to their own but do not try to convert those who are happy with their own religion.

RELATIONSHIP WITH OTHER RELIGIONS: Buddha taught that there is a path to enlightenment for each of us, including non-Buddhist paths. However, when any religion claims itself as the only way to enlightment, the Buddhist says that this is attachment to ideas. True insight is not to be confused with conceptual knowledge or perverted views.

CHURCH OF PERFECT LIBERTY 700 South Adams Street Glendale, California 91205	Rev. Kingo Inamura (Oya) Director of North American Mission

HISTORICAL ROOTS: In 1912, Tokumitsu Kanada, a Shinto priest and ascetic, founded the Tokumitsu-Kyo. One of Kanada's disciples was Miki Tokuhara, a former Zen Buddhist priest. After the death of Kanada in 1919, Miki planted a shrub, called himorogi, and "worshiped" it for five years as Kanada had instructed him. In 1924, Miki received the new revelation which Kanada had promised, and founded Hito no Michi Kyodan (The Way of Man). Hito no Michi, which emphasized the reality of both art and nature, met with considerable success in Japan. In 1937, however, it was prohibited by the Japanese military government. Miki was arrested and died in prison in 1938. Miki's son, Tokuchika, became the leader of Hito no Michi until 1943, when the Japanese Supreme Court upheld the prohibition and Hito no Michi was disbanded. In 1946, Tokuchika and other leaders of Hito no Michi formed the Perfect Liberty Kyodan (Church of Perfect Liberty).

CURRENT WORLD LEADER: Tokuchika Miki, the Oshieoya (Father of the Teachings).

ORIGINS IN THE U.S.: In 1957, several lay missionaries began work in the U.S., and the first Perfect Liberty minister arrived in 1960.

NUMBER OF ADHERENTS IN THE U.S.: 50,000 Families.

ORGANIZATIONAL STRUCTURE: Oshieoya (the Patriarch) is the sole and supreme authority in PL. Ministers achieving a certain enlightenment and state of mind are selected, designated Yuso (disciples) and granted the title "Oya." The succession of the Patriarch is assured and continuous. The successor is chosen from among the Yusos and elevated and trained.

CHURCH OF PERFECT LIBERTY	Page 2
Leadership, Worship	

LEADERSHIP AND ROLE OF MINISTERS: PL ministers administrate churches, educate members in faithful living, minister to their spiritual needs and function as leaders of the congregations. Their main duty is to convey the teachings of PL to members and non-members alike. PL ministers are obligated to perform Divine Rites, Services, Ceremonies, all ritual and devotions wherever they are stationed. They are invested with authority for their particular mission by the Patriarch. Once ordained, they are solely responsible to the Patriarch.

WHO MAY CONDUCT WORSHIP SERVICE? Any minister, church assistant, or qualified member.

IS GROUP WORSHIP REQUIRED? Yes, although a member unable to attend services may conduct an abbreviated authorized version of the service alone, with his family, or with other members if he has a portable or family shrine.

WORSHIP REQUIREMENTS: Morning and Evening Services in the member's home. Participation in the monthly Thanksgiving Ceremony (21st of the month) and the ceremonies for the four annual festivals (see "Holidays") is required. Attendance at other Services is recommended, not required.

MINIMUM EQUIPMENT FOR WORSHIP: (1) Portable Shrine (Omitama), 4" high, 2" diameter, in a leather case; (2) PL Prayer Book (Kyoten); (3) Book of Divine Instructions (Mioshie); (4) Envelope for Offerings (Hosho).

FACILITIES FOR WORSHIP: Churches or designated chapels. Members unable to attend a church may perform services and ceremonies at home or other suitable location using a family or portable shrine as an altar.

CHURCH OF PERFECT LIBERTY	Page 3
Requirements	

OTHER SPECIFIC RELIGIOUS REQUIREMENTS OTHER THAN WORSHIP: Visitations to
   churches or chapels, attendance at meetings, classes and seminars,
   devotional service (including physical labor, propagation and teaching),
   Divine Service (including officiating at services), conducting special
   prayers (Oyashikiri) and making pilgrimages when prescribed, caring for
   other members, making contributions, pledges, and monthly offerings
   (Hosho, Shikirikin, Gokafu) to the Church.

DIETARY LAWS OR RESTRICTIONS: Generally none, except when prescribed by a
   physician. The church's teachings advise practice of "Healthful Living"
   and moderation. Many members, therefore, abstain from the use of tobacco and alcohol, or some may be vegetarians.

SPECIAL RELIGIOUS HOLIDAYS: The 21st of each month is a "Thanksgiving" day,
   with special ceremonies held in each PL Church. There are also four
   annual festivals, including Founder's Day (Kyoso Sai, August 1),
   Oshieoya's Tanjo Sai Birthday (April 8), New Year's Day (January 1),
   and PL Establishment Day (PL Sai, September 29).

FUNERAL AND BURIAL REQUIREMENTS: A matter of the individual choice. If
   the deceased has made his wishes known, his family would make those
   decisions after consulting a minister. A minister must conduct burial
   or cremation service, the funeral service, and assist the family with
   the disposition of the remains.

AUTOPSY: May be performed when needed. However, permission from the family
   should be obtained, if possible.

CHURCH OF PERFECT LIBERTY	Page 4
Requirements, Position on Service, Basic Beliefs	

MEDICAL TREATMENT: Generally no restrictions, when performed by competent
authorities.

UNIFORM APPEARANCE REQUIREMENT: Members are required to wear an amulet
(blessed by the Patriarch for bodily protection), usually a ring or pen-
dant, at all times. PL badges are worn on an outer garment over the
left side of the chest as a visible expression of faith, and most
members wear them at all times.

POSITION ON SERVICE IN THE ARMED FORCES: Service to one's country and to
humanity as a whole is a cornerstone of PL Faith. The Church encourages
members to be of service wherever and whenever needed. Due, however, to
the basic pacifistic nature of the teachings and PL's vigorous efforts
to bring about World Peace, if a PL member does seek exemption or non-
combatant status, the Church and its teachings will support his claims
and rights.

ANY OTHER PRACTICES OR TEACHINGS WHICH MAY CONFLICT WITH MILITARY DIRECTIVES
OR PRACTICES: None.

IS A MINISTER REQUIRED AT TIME DEATH? A minister must be at hand to care
for the final rites, needs of the member, and to conduct the special
ceremony held within 24 hours after death, before the funeral.

BASIC TEACHINGS OR BELIEFS: (1) Life is Art. (2) Man's life is a succession
of self-expressions. (3) Man is a manifestation of God. (4) Man suf-
fers if he fails to express himself. (5) Man loses his true self when
swayed by feelings and emotions. (6) Man's true self is revealed when
his ego is effaced. (7) All things exist in mutual relationship to one

BELIEFS (continued): another. (8) Live radiantly as the sun. (9) All men
are equal. (10) Strive for creating mutual happiness. (11) Have true
faith in God. (12) There is a way (function) peculiar to every "name"
(existence). (13) There is a way for men, and there is another for
women. (14) All is for world peace. (15) All is a mirror. (16) All
things progress and develop. (17) Comprehend what is most essential.
(18) At every moment man stands at the crossroads of good and evil.
(19) Act when your intuition dictates. (20) Live in perfect union of
mind and matter. (21) Live in Perfect Liberty.

CREEDAL STATEMENTS AND/OR AUTHORITATIVE LITERATURE: The PL Creed: "(1) I
live for the joy of an artistic life. (2) I pray for the happiness of
others. (3) I live with true effort and sincerity. (4) I maintain the
highest dignity and honor. (5) I strive for the great peace of the
world."

The PL Declaration: "Life is Art. Man realizes life's true beauty,
charm and meaning only when he lives an artistic life. Then, what is an
artistic life? It is to freely express one's individuality in his particular field of work. However, one's true individuality cannot be
expressed to the highest degree unless one is completely free of egois-
tic interest and selfish gains. One must live in a state of objectivity,
expressing one's individuality in the interest and welfare of all mankind. We, members of PL, hereby declare to live an artistic life, de-
taching ourselves from egocentricity and expressing our individuality in
complete freedom and spontaneousness. We, members of PL, also declare

CHURCH OF PERFECT LIBERTY	Page 6
Literature, Ethics, Recruiting, Relationships	

LITERATURE (continued): that it is our duty to propagate and implant the teachings of PL to the world and we shall contribute to the world community of men."

    Since the sole authority for all Divine Rites, teachings, activities, devotions and functions of PL is invested by God to the Patriarch, PL holds all of the Patriarch's writings, books, articles, sermons, lectures and sayings as authoritative.

ETHICAL PRACTICES: PL teachings require members to abide by and uphold "the Law of the Land," and to live in strict accordance with PL teachings.

HOW DOES PL RECRUIT MEMBERS? Members are encouraged to vigorously share their experiences and to invite individuals to attend PL meetings and services. Members also distribute church literature, and the church sponsors a number of public festivals.

RELATIONSHIP WITH OTHER RELIGIONS: In general, PL cooperates in any activity that will bring about religious unity, social harmony or in any way will alleviate suffering. Many PL members belong to other churches or practice the teachings of another religion.

NICHIREN SHOSHU ACADEMY 525 Wilshire Boulevard P.O. Box 1427 Santa Monica, California 90406	George M. Williams General Director AKA: NSA; Soka Gakkai

HISTORICAL ROOTS: Nichiren Shoshu is a school of Buddhism which traces its lineage to Gautama Buddha (1029-949 B.C.) and which was formally established in Japan by Nichiren Daishonin (1222-1282 A.D.) who based his enlightenment on the Lotus Sutra of Gautama. The Head Temple of Nichiren Shoshu remained relatively uninfluential until 1930 when the Nichiren Shoshu Soka Gakkai, a lay organization, was begun and has since grown to a membership of nearly 20 million persons practicing this life-philosophy in 80 different nations.

CURRENT WORLD LEADER: Daisaku Ikeda, President, Nichiren Shoshu Soka Gakkai.

ORIGINS IN THE U.S.: George M. Williams, currently General Director of NSA, immigrated to the U.S. from Japan in 1957 and began contacting persons who had been members in Japan. Many non-orientals adopted the beliefs during a major growth period between 1965-70.

NUMBER OF ADHERENTS IN THE U.S.: Approximately 235,000.

ORGANIZATIONAL STRUCTURE: A highly-developed series of communication links designed to provide guidance of President Ikeda together with the fundamentals of the religious practice and tradition to members and interested guests. Organizational direction provided by the General Director, and the NSA Executive Planning Board. Basic activities are discussion meetings held in private homes, consisting of 10-20 members who complete the evening worship together, share experiences with the practice and study the history and philosophy of the religion. In areas having major concentrations of members, community centers exist.

Leadership, Worship

LEADERSHIP AND ROLE OF PRIESTS: The functions of maintaining the orthodoxy

   of the teachings and protecting its relics are assumed by the priesthood,

   centering on the High Priest at the Head Temple in Japan.

      Weddings, funerals, meetings, and other routine religious functions

   are officiated by senior members of the organization.

      The Gohonzon, the object of worship which is accorded the respect

   due the enlightened life of the universe it represents, is inscribed

   under the authority of each successive high priest and is provided to

   each member of the religion.

WHO MAY CONDUCT WORSHIP SERVICES? Daily worship is completed on an indivi-

   dual basis by each member, but may be performed whenever a group is

   assembled.

IS GROUP WORSHIP REQUIRED? Not on a regular basis, although participation

   in discussion meetings is strongly recommended, both as an encouragement

   to individual practice and as a means of attracting new members.

WORSHIP REQUIREMENTS: Daily recitation of portions of the Lotus Sutra

   (Gongyo) both morning and evening accompanied by the repeated invocation

   of Nam-myoho-renge-kyo which is performed before the Gohonzon, a scroll

   measuring approximately 10 x 20 inches. Tradition demands that the

   Gohonzon be appropriately enshrined in an altar and that the altar also

   contain offerings of water, fruit, evergreen, candles, and incense. The

   worshiper would use prayer beads and a bell during the service.

NICHIREN SHOSHU ACADEMY   Page 3

Requirements, Position on Service

MINIMUM EQUIPMENT FOR WORSHIP: The Gohonzon, which represents the entity of
    life itself, suitably enshrined in a protected area. The scroll may be
    rolled up after each worship service, although this would be appropri-
    ate only in the most difficult circumstances.

OTHER SPECIFIC RELIGIOUS REQUIREMENTS OTHER THAN WORSHIP: None, other than
    to protect the Gohonzon.

DIETARY LAWS OR RESTRICTIONS: None.

SPECIAL RELIGIOUS HOLIDAYS: None which require special observances.

FUNERAL AND BURIAL REQUIREMENTS: Individual choice; cremation preferred.

AUTOPSY: No restrictions.

CREMATION: Preferred, but not required.

MEDICAL TREATMENT: No restrictions.

UNIFORM OR APPEARANCE REQUIREMENTS: None. Members may choose to carry
    Gohonzon scroll and prayer beads on their person, especially during
    military action.

POSITION ON SERVICE IN THE ARMED FORCES: No restrictions; individual prefer-
    ence is honored. Military service is considered a patriotic duty and,
    although a fundamental respect for human life is cherished, there is
    no compunction about obedience to lawful military directives.

IS A PRIEST OR LAY MINISTER REQUIRED AT TIME OF DEATH? No.

ANY OTHER PRACTICES OR TEACHINGS WHICH MAY CONFLICT WITH MILITARY DIRECTIVES
    OR PRACTICES: None.

NICHIREN SHOSHU ACADEMY	Page 4
Literature, Basic Beliefs	

CREEDAL STATEMENTS AND/OR AUTHORITATIVE LITERATURE: The Gosho, collected
   writings of Nichiren Daishonin; and expositions on the practical application of the philosophy authored by Daisaku Ikeda and other lay leaders,
   including NSA periodicals, the World Tribune newspaper, and the NSA
   Quarterly magazine.

BASIC TEACHINGS AND BELIEFS: NSA believes that each person can attain "enlightenment" or the universality of life within himself/herself. Happiness is a birthright and can be achieved by being in harmony with the
   universal law which is Nam-myoho-renge-kyo. The individual is viewed
   as an integral part of his/her environment, so that conditions in the
   world are mirror images of the human condition itself. Thus happiness
   and peace can be obtained by chanting Nam-myoho-renge-kyo and reciting
   the Lotus Sutra (Gongyo).

   The philosophy stresses cause and effect, and chanting Nam-myoho-
   renge-kyo is considered the highest and most effective cause to change
   any condition. Karma, or destiny, is the result of the individual's
   own past actions and can only be changed by making the proper causes.
   The ultimate goal of the religion is both universal and specific. While
   attaining his/her own enlightenment or "human revolution," each member
   is achieving harmony with his/her surroundings and contributing to a
   better world.

NICHIREN SHOSHU ACADEMY   Page 5

Ethics, Recruiting, Relationships

ETHICAL PRACTICES: No specific set of ethical practices is prescribed for

    members other than common sense and the accepted standards of social

    conduct which are applicable to the land in which they live. NSA

    teaches that a code of ethics must be developed by the individual as

    a result of his/her practice of the philosophy and personal character

    development.

HOW DOES NSA RECRUIT MEMBERS: *Proselytizing* is done on a person-to-person

    basis and is considered a fundamental practice of the religion. Friends

    and associates are invited to attend a discussion meeting and encouraged

    to attempt the practice, without any prerequisite of faith. Membership

    is formalized by completing a written application and undergoing a

    conversion (Gojukai) ceremony during which the person would receive

    his/her own Gohonzon.

RELATIONSHIPS TO OTHER RELIGIONS: NSA believes that its underlying philos-

    ophy is compatible with other non-Buddhist religions, that its practice

    is simply an extension of those of the more familiar Judaeo-Christian

    heritage of the U.S. It does teach that other sects of Buddhism are

    provisional and not correct for the modern era but is strongly com-

    mitted to the principle of granting freedom of religion to all.

        Nichiren Shoshu, among all Buddhist schools, promises that each

    person has the immediate potential for enlightenment in this lifetime,

    regardless of past causes, only through the basic practice to the

    Gohonzon.

NICHIREN SHOSHU ACADEMY   Page 6

Relationships

RELATIONSHIP WITH OTHER RELIGIONS (continued): "Buddhism is simply humanism --

    not the academic humanism of early Western scholars in the fifteenth cen-

    tury, but humanism which embodies a philosophy that leads to happiness,

    both individually and in the social context." (From NSA Handbook No. 2:

    The Buddhist Tradition, World Tribune Press, Santa Monica, California,

    1972, page 3.)

INTRODUCTION: JEWISH GROUPS

Judaism is the oldest of the three major western religions, and is the forerunner of both Christianity and Islam. The history of Judaism is well known, chronicled first in the Bible and later in rabbinic literature.

Unlike Christianity, Judaism reflects a remarkable unanimity among its various groups in terms of organization, beliefs, and requirements. In many instances, differences are a matter of degree rather than of substantial disagreement. Nevertheless, differences do exist - even to the extent that there is not a general agreement as to how divided Judaism really is.

The three largest groups within Judaism are the Conservative, Orthodox, and Reform bodies. These groups are generally seen as the major Jewish "denominations," and Jewish military chaplains are apportioned between them. From this perspective, other groups can be viewed as related to one of these three. However, some other groups, such as the Reconstructionist Jews, tend to see themselves as a separate branch of Judaism. Reconstructionists, therefore, refer to the "four major branches of Judaism," rather than three. Within the three largest groups there may also be subdivisions which will arise. There are differences, for example between Orthodox Jews who follow the Ashkenazic rite (from Jeremiah 51:27) and those who follow the Sephardic rite (from Obadiah 20). Ethnic differences may also exist, in that Ashkenazic rites were largely followed among Germanic Jews, while Jews of Spanish and Portugese descent have largely observed the Sephardic rite.

Black Jews, including the Black Hebrew Israelite Nation, trace their history through more than 2,500 years of Judaism in Africa. Other racial or ethnic variations also exist.

In general, however, Judaism remains relatively constant in terms of basic beliefs and practices, and most American Jews will be identified with the traditions represented in this section.

BLACK HEBREW ISRAELITE NATION
c/o B'Nai Zaken
4233 South Indiana
Chicago, Illinois 60653

Levi Ben Israel

AKA: Black Jews

HISTORICAL ROOTS: The Black Hebrew Israelite Nation traces its roots to the
Torah. They believe themselves to be the true descendants of the orig-
inal Jews and heirs of the Promised land, as are all black people.
After the destruction of the second temple of Jerusalem, any Israelites
remaining are believed to have moved southward and settled in Africa.
Hundreds of years later, descendants of these Israelites were sold into
slavery by members of the indigenous population and finally shipped to
America, still conscious of their Israelite identity.

As early as 1880, some black people began to recover their identity
as Israelites, aided in part by the rediscovery of the Falashas, people
in central Africa believed to be descendants of King Solomon and the
Queen of Sheba. The Falashas have practiced Judaism since 600 B.C.

CURRENT WORLD LEADER: None generally recognized by all groups. Local congregations are independent and self-governing.

ORIGINS IN THE U.S.: First gathered in the 1960s, primarily among black
people in Chicago and other urban centers. Ben Ami and Moreh Isedek led
a group in migrating to Liberia in 1967 and to Israel in 1971. Most of
these later returned to the U.S. Other groups, not a part of the migra-
tion, remained as independent congregations in various cities.

NUMBER OF ADHERENTS IN THE U.S.: Uncertain. Believed to be about 4,000.

ORGANIZATIONAL STRUCTURE: Independent local congregations exist in Chicago,
Cincinnati, Philadelphia, Newark, New York, and Boston, led by their own
religious teachers or rabbis. Currently, there is no central organization, and wide variations exist among local groups.

LEADERSHIP AND ROLE OF RABBIS: As with other Jewish groups, the role of a

    rabbi is inherent in the name - teacher. Rabbis lead the local congre-

    gation in religious practices and worship, provide counsel and guidance.

WHO MAY CONDUCT SERVICES? Any member, but usually a rabbi (teacher).

IS GROUP WORSHIP REQUIRED? Yes. Judaism is characterized by its group na-

    ture. Sabbath worship is a requirement for all members.

WORSHIP REQUIREMENTS: In accordance with the Torah, both group and private

    worship are encouraged. The Jew is to approach God with clean hands,

    a pure heart, and prayers must be sincere and devoted.

MINIMUM EQUIPMENT FOR WORSHIP: A copy of the Torah (law) and songbooks.

FACILITIES FOR WORSHIP: Generally a synagogue containing the Torah.

DIETARY LAWS OR RESTRICTIONS: In keeping with the Torah and Jewish tradi-

    tion, pork and its derivatives are forbidden, as is any form of meat

    with blood content present. All food must be kosher (i.e., blessed by

    a rabbi or teacher).

SPECIAL RELIGIOUS HOLIDAYS: The Hebrew Israelites keep the Sabbath and all

    the feast days common to Judaism -- the Passover and the Day of Atone-

    ment, and the Feast of Tabernacles. While in Liberia, the Passover was

    celebrated with the sacrifice of a lamb. These celebrations are figured

    on a lunar calendar, and vary from year to year.

FUNERAL AND BURIAL REQUIREMENTS: Specific requirements are uncertain

    and should be assisted by a rabbi.

AUTOPSY: Generally prohibited except in special circumstances.

Requirements, Position on Service, Beliefs, Literature, Ethics

CREMATION: In general, cremation is prohibited by Jewish law.

MEDICAL TREATMENT: No restrictions.

UNIFORM APPEARANCE REQUIREMENTS: None.

POSITION ON SERVICE IN THE ARMED FORCES: None, except where it might
    interfere with the Sabbath or Jewish holidays.

IS A RABBI OR TEACHER REQUIRED AT TIME OF DEATH? Not required, but desira-
    ble.

ANY OTHER PRACTICES OR TEACHINGS WHICH MAY CONFLICT WITH MILITARY DIRECTIVES
    OR PRACTICE: None.

BASIC TEACHINGS OR BELIEFS: The Hebrew Israelite Nation follows closely the
    faith of their ancestors Abraham, Isaac, and Jacob. They affirm belief
    in Jehovah, the One God of Israel. They believe that black people are
    the descendants of the Patriarchs of what is commonly called the Old
    Testament. They observe the Sabbath and the Jewish holidays.

CREEDAL STATEMENTS AND/OR AUTHORITATIVE LITERATURE: The holy book of the
    Hebrew Israelites is the Torah, which contains the Law as revealed and
    handed down through Moses. Authoritative information on Black Jews can
    be found in two books: Black Hebrew Israelites: From America to the
    Promised Land by Shaleak ben Jehuda (Vantage Press) and From Babylon
    to Timbuktu by Rudolph R. Winsor (Exposition Press).

ETHICAL PRACTICES: Dress properly and clean. Exemplify piousness by re-
    fraining from the use of foul language. Respect the personhood of
    others. Be peaceful.

BLACK HEBREW ISRAELITE NATION   Page 4

Recruiting, Relationships

HOW DOES THE HEBREW ISRAELITE NATION RECRUIT MEMBERS? By word of mouth,

    as there is no formal recruitment program. All *proselytizing* is

    among black people and aimed at awakening them to their true

    identity as Jews.

RELATIONSHIPS WITH OTHER RELIGIONS: Generally cordial, but primary focus is

    on work within the black community.

CONSERVATIVE JUDAISM   Rabbi Stanley Rabinowitz
The Rabbinical Assembly
3080 Broadway
New York, New York 10027

HISTORICAL ROOTS: Judaism's earliest history is chronicled in the Bible and
its subsequent development is detailed in the vast, post-Biblical rabbinic literature. Of the three major branches in Judaism today, Conservative Judaism, which began in the middle of the 19th century,
opposes extreme changes in traditional practice but does permit certain
modifications in observance. The Reconstructionist Movement, a deri-
vative of Conservative Judaism, was inspired by the teaching and writings of Mordecai Kaplan, particularly his Judaism as a Civilization,
published in 1935.

CURRENT WORLD LEADERS: Judaism has no single world leader. Conservative
Jewish congregations constitute autonomous religious communities, each
of which elects its own rabbinic and lay leadership.

ORIGINS IN THE U.S.: The Conservative movement in the U.S. began as a reaction against the radical stand of the Reform Rabbis at the Pittsburgh
Conference in 1885. Rabbi Sabato Morais, leader of the dissenting
group, helped organize the Jewish Theological Seminary in New York in
1886. It was, however, Solomon Schechter, called to head the Jewish
Theological Seminary in 1902, who became the acknowledged leader and
spokesman of Conservative Judaism. In 1935, a number of students and
followers of Mordecai Kaplan's views initiated the Reconstructionist
movement (see Historical Roots.)

NUMBER OF ADHERENTS IN THE U.S.: Of an estimated total Jewish population
in excess of 5,000,000 in the U.S., those who have some formal affiliation with a Conservative congregation total approximately 1,500,000.

CONSERVATIVE JUDAISM	Page 2

Organization, Leaders, Worship

ORGANIZATIONAL STRUCTURE: The national organization, numbering approximately 824 member congregations, is the United Synagogue of America. Its auxiliary organizations are the Women's League of the United Synagogue established in 1918 (now called the Women's League for Conservative Judaism); the United Synagogue Youth, successor to the Young People's League of the United Synagogue, organized in 1921; and the Federation of Men's Clubs, formed in 1929. The Jewish Theological Seminary (J.T.S.) founded in 1866 is the Conservative rabbinical school. The Rabbinical Assembly began as a J.T.S. alumni association, but now includes Conservative rabbis who are not graduates of the J.T.S.

LEADERSHIP AND ROLE OF RABBIS: Within Judaism, the priestly function is not vested in any one individual or group. The rabbi is the appointed spiritual leader who guides and represents the congregation. In addition, there are elected lay leaders, both in the congregation and in the larger Jewish community.

WHO MAY CONDUCT WORSHIP SERVICES? Any knowledgeable Jew.

IS GROUP WORSHIP REQUIRED? Yes. What is distinctive about Jewish worship is its congregational or group character. Congregational worship has led to the adoption of certain conventions, such as the "minyan" or ten men who constitute the minimum number for holding public worship.

WORSHIP REQUIREMENTS: Although there are fixed times for public worship, the Jew finds ample opportunity in daily life to offer thanks and praise to God. The only requirement for private as for public worship is that a

CONSERVATIVE JUDAISM	Page 3
Worship, Requirements	

WORSHIP REQUIREMENTS (continued) Jew approach God with "clean hands and a

   pure heart," that the prayers be prompted by sincerity and integrity.

MINIMUM EQUIPMENT FOR WORSHIP: The Torah or the Scroll of the Law and its

   accouterments, prayer books, Hebrew Bible, skull-caps, and prayer shawls.

FACILITIES FOR WORSHIP: In addition to providing the ark to house the Torah

   and adequate storage space for the above enumerated equipment, the

   facility for worship should be in keeping with the solemn dignity of

   the activity of prayer.

OTHER SPECIFIC RELIGIOUS REQUIREMENTS OTHER THAN WORSHIP: Judaism requires

   that all aspects of life be santified. Since the vertical relationship

   between man and God is paralleled by a horizontal relationship between

   man and man, the same honesty and sincerity which is required in one

   relationship is also required in the other.

DIETARY LAWS OR RESTRICTIONS: The dietary laws constitute a sizeable litera-

   ture, beginning with the Biblical prohibitions in Leviticus 11 and Deute-

   ronomy 14. These were later expanded considerably by rabbinic inter-

   pretation and include, among other things, the prohibitions against

   eating the flesh of certain animals and against the mixing of milk and

   meat.

SPECIAL RELIGIOUS HOLIDAYS: In addition to the Sabbath, religious holidays

   include the three Biblical pilgrimage festivals, Passover, Pentecost, and

   Tabernacles - and the New Year and Day of Atonement. The first and last

   days of Passover and Tabernacles are considered days of obligation (i.e.,

Requirements, Position on Service

SPECIAL RELIGIOUS HOLIDAYS (continued): no work is permitted), but the inter-

mediate days are not. The Sabbath and the Day of Atonement are also days

of obligation on which all manner of work is forbidden. On the other

holidays, fire may be used, vital food may be prepared, and carrying is

permitted. All holidays (except the Day of Atonement) are observed for

two days. The post-Biblical festivals of Hanukkah and Purim do not con-

stitute days of obligation.

FUNERAL AND BURIAL REQUIREMENTS: The purpose of Jewish funeral and burial

requirements is both to honor the deceased and to provide comfort to

the mourners. The requirements include ritual cleansing of the body,

clothing the body in white linen, shrouds and prayer shawl, and the

use of a simple wooden coffin. The funeral service is simple and

prescribed by Jewish law. Following the burial, close relatives

observe a mourning period which is normally seven days.

AUTOPSY: Permitted when the health of the community is benefited, the ends

of justice are promoted, or medical science is advanced.

CREMATION: Not permitted. Burial in the earth is required.

MEDICAL TREATMENT: Jews have always held physicians in great esteem as in-

struments through whom God could effect a cure. Good health is consid-

ered both an individual obligation and a group responsibility, and med-

ical treatment is one means to help achieve good health.

UNIFORM APPEARANCE REQUIREMENTS: None.

POSITION ON SERVICE IN THE ARMED FORCES: As early as the colonial period Jews

served in the militia. During the War of Independence and in all

CONSERVATIVE JUDAISM   Page 5

Position on Service, Beliefs, Literature

POSITION OF SERVICE IN THE ARMED FORCES (continued): subsequent wars, Jews
    have served in the armed forces as a necessary act of defending their
    country and of helping to maintain it free and strong.

IS A RABBI REQUIRED AT THE TIME OF DEATH? Anyone in the presence of a dying
    person may guide him in the expression of Vidui (confession) and the
    affirmation of faith (the Sh'ma), but the presence of a rabbi is impor-
    tant both for guidance and consolation.

ANY OTHER PRACTICES OR TEACHINGS WHICH MAY CONFLICT WITH MILITARY DIRECTIVES
    OR PRACTICES: While the basic philosophy of Judaism is the sanctifica-
    tion of life, it recognizes the necessity to preserve and defend one's
    country, without which the "sanctification of life" becomes a meaning-
    less phrase.

BASIC TEACHINGS OR BELIEFS: Judaism is a religion based on progressive reve-
    lation; at the core of this revelation is the doctrine of ethical mono-
    theism. The Everliving God and Infinite Creator is both transcendent
    and immanent; He is omnipresent, omnipotent, and omniscient. He hears
    prayer, and the pure in heart may commune with Him directly without any
    intercession. Man is free and is not tainted with Original Sin. Juda-
    ism affirms life as good and seeks to endow it with spiritual and moral
    worth. The Jewish affirmation of faith emphasizes God's unity and is
    expressed in the Sh'ma: "Hear, O Israel, The Lord Our God, The Lord is
    One."

CREEDAL STATEMENTS AND/OR AUTHORITATIVE LITERATURE: Judaism is a religion of
    deed rather than creed. The deeds required of a Jew are both ritual and

CONSERVATIVE JUDAISM   Page 6

Literature, Ethics, Recruiting, Relationships

LITERATURE (continued): ethical, the former in relation to God and the lat-
     ter in relation to one's fellowman. Authoritative Jewish literature
     includes the Bible, the Talmud, the Responsa literature, and the Codes.
     The most authoritative Code is the Shulhan Arukh by Joseph Caro. In Con-
     servative Judaism, the process of legal interpretation of Jewish law and
     ritual is vested in the Law Committee of the Rabbinical Assembly which,
     by discussion and vote in the spirit of the traditional process, pre-
     serves the viability and adaptability of Jewish law to contemporary life.

ETHICAL PRACTICES: Ethics is inseparable from religion in Judaism, and the
     deepest concern of the Torah in its broadest sense is morality, both in-
     dividual and social.

HOW DOES CONSERVATIVE JUDAISM RECRUIT MEMBERS? Membership in Judaism is pri-
     marily through birth to a Jewish mother. In addition, although Judaism
     is not a *proselytizing* religion, it does have procedures for conversion
     to Judaism of those who freely and of their own accord seek to embrace
     it.

RELATIONSHIP TO OTHER RELIGIONS: Throughout its venerable history, Judaism
     has come in contact with many peoples, religions, and creeds. It has
     both influenced and been influenced by them; yet it has ever retained its
     religious and cultural uniqueness and has remained true to the principles
     of ethical monotheism. Judaism does not seek to supplant other reli-
     gions, but rather to labor with them in honorable fellowship to bring
     about universal peace and justice on earth.

ORTHODOX JUDAISM   Rabbi Israel Klavan
Rabbinical Council of America
220 Park Avenue, South
New York, New York 10003

HISTORICAL ROOTS: The early history of Judaism is chronicled in the Bible

and its subsequent development is detailed in the vast, post-Biblical

rabbinic literature. Of the three major branches of Judaism today,

Orthodox Judaism is that which subscribes to the belief in the Divine

Revelation of Torah Law and its principles through Moses and insists

upon strict adherence to these laws as codified in the Shulhan Aruch

(Code of Jewish Law) and their application to contemporary life as

interpreted by leading rabbinic authorities.

CURRENT WORLD LEADERS: Judaism has no single world leader. Leading rabbinic

authorities are looked to, however, for direction. Orthodox Jewish

congregations are autonomous religious communities, each of which elects

its own rabbinic and lay leadership (see also "Organization").

ORIGINS IN THE U.S.: Judaism came to the U.S. with the first Jewish settlers

as early as the first quarter of the 17th century. In 1730, the first

synagogue was built in New York and others followed soon after. These

early synagogues followed the Sephardic rite. In 1801, however, the

first synagogue to follow the Ashkenazic rite was organized as Rodef

Shalom in Philadelphia. Until 1824, when Reform Judaism began in

Charleston, South Carolina, all congregations were Orthodox.

NUMBER OF ADHERENTS IN THE U.S.: Of an estimated total Jewish population of

5,732,000 in the U.S., those who have some formal affiliation with an

Orthodox congregation total in excess of 1,000,000.

ORGANIZATIONAL STRUCTURE: The majority of Orthodox Jews are organized

locally rather than nationally. However, the Union of Orthodox Jewish

ORTHODOX JUDAISM	Page 2

Organization, Leaders, Worship

ORGANIZATION (continued): Congregations represents about 1,000 member congregations and was founded in New York City in 1898. Among other Orthodox Institutions are YESHIVOS Seminaries of Torah Study, including the Isaac Elchanan Theological Seminary and Yeshiva University; the Hebrew Theological College in Chicago, the Ner Israel Rabbinical College in Baltimore, Yeshiva Torah Vadath, and Hayim Berlin in New York. Orthodox rabbis are represented by the Rabbinical Council of America and other established rabbinical associations.

LEADERSHIP AND ROLE OF RABBIS: A rabbi is the appointed spiritual leader who guides and represents the congregation. In addition, there are elected lay leaders, both in the congregation and in the Jewish community.

WHO MAY CONDUCT WORSHIP SERVICES? Any observant and knowledgeable Jew may conduct worship services.

IS GROUP WORSHIP REQUIRED? Yes. What is distinctive about Jewish worship is its congregational or group character. Congregational worship has led to the adoption of certain conventions, such as the "minyan" or quorum of ten men who constitute the minimum number for public worship.

WORSHIP REQUIREMENTS: There are fixed times for public worship -- three times daily, morning, afternoon, and evening. A minyan or quorum of ten males, as mentioned above, is required. When the minyan is not available, individuals must privately worship, offering thanks and praise to God. A Jew must approach God with clean hands and a pure heart, with prayers prompted by a sincere and devoted heart.

ORTHODOX JUDAISM	Page 3

Worship, Requirements

MINIMUM EQUIPMENT FOR WORSHIP: The Torah or the Scroll of the Law and its accouterments, prayer books, Hebrew Bible, skull-caps, prayer shawls, and tfilin *(phylacteries)*, which are to be worn by males at morning prayer (except on the Sabbath). (Male Jews are required to keep their heads covered.)

FACILITIES FOR WORSHIP: A synagogue, usually oriented to the East so that worshipers can pray facing Jerusalem. Every synagogue contains the ark which houses the Torah and adequate storage space for worship equipment. Also, in the event a synagogue is not available and some other building is used instead, non-Jewish symbols should be absent from the facility, at least while it is being used for worship by Jews.

OTHER SPECIFIC RELIGIOUS REQUIREMENTS OTHER THAN WORSHIP: Judaism requires that all aspects of life be sanctified. Since the vertical relationship between man and God is paralleled by a horizontal relationship between man and man, the same honesty and sincerity which is required in the one relationship is also required in the other.

DIETARY LAWS OR RESTRICTIONS: Dietary laws, beginning with Leviticus 11 and Deuteronomy 14, contain prohibitions against animals that do not have split hooves and chew their cud, sea food without fins and scales; cooking milk and meat together, and certain fowl. These laws are amplified by the oral law to include the complete separation of milk and meat, including the use of separate utensils for each. All permissible fowl and cattle must be ritually slaughtered.

ORTHODOX JUDAISM   Page 4

Requirements

SPECIAL RELIGIOUS HOLIDAYS: In addition to the Sabbath, religious holidays

include the three Biblical pilgrimage festivals -- Passover, Pentecost,

and Tabernacles and the New Year (Rosh Hashanah) and the Day of Atone-

ment (Yom Kippur). All holidays except the Day of Atonement are ob-

served for two days. The first two and last two days of Passover and

Tabernacles are days on which work is forbidden. All manner of work is

forbidden on the Sabbath as well as on holidays. The preparation of

food is prohibited only on the Sabbath and the Day of Atonement. Han-

ukkah and Purim are post-Biblical holidays, and do not include a pro-

hibition against work.

FUNERAL AND BURIAL REQUIREMENTS: The purpose of Jewish funeral and burial

requirements is both to honor the deceased and to provide comfort to the

mourners. The requirements include ritual cleansing of the body, cloth-

ing the body in white shrouds and prayer shawl, and the use of a simple

wooden coffin. The funeral service is simple and prescribed by Jewish

law. Following the burial, close relatives observe a mourning period

(shiva) which is seven days.

AUTOPSY: Not permitted except in very unusual circumstances (e.g., promoting

justice), because of prohibitions against mutilation of the body and

disrespect for the dead. A rabbi should be consulted before autopsy.

CREMATION: Prohibited. Burial in the earth is required.

MEDICAL TREATMENT: No restrictions. Jews consider physicians as instruments

through whom God can effect a cure. Medical treatment is viewed as one

means to help achieve good health.

ORTHODOX JUDAISM   Page 5

Position on Service, Beliefs

POSITION ON SERVICE IN THE ARMED FORCES: In every U.S. war, Jews have

    served in the armed forces as a necessary act of defending their

    country and of helping to maintain it free and strong.

IS A RABBI REQUIRED AT THE TIME OF DEATH? Anyone in the presence of a dying

    person may guide him in the expression of Vidui (confession) and the

    affirmation of faith (the Sh'ma), but the presence of a rabbi is im-

    portant both for guidance and consolation.

ANY OTHER PRACTICES OR TEACHINGS WHICH MAY CONFLICT WITH MILITARY DIRECTIVES

    OR PRACTICE: While the basic philosophy of Judaism is the sanctifica-

    tion of life, it recognizes the necessity to preserve and defend one's

    country, without which the "sanctification of life" becomes a meaning-

    less phrase.

BASIC TEACHINGS OR BELIEFS: Based on belief in one God, Creator of the uni-

    verse, who revealed His divine pattern for life for all mankind through

    the Torah, given to Moses and the Jewish people at Mount Sinai. Commit-

    ment to these laws contained in the written and oral Torah transcends

    time, place, or circumstance unless specifically provided. The ever-

    living God and Infinite Creator is both transcendent and immanent; He

    is omnipresent, omnipotent, and omniscient. He hears prayer, and the

    pure in heart may commune with Him directly without any intercessor.

    Man is free and is not tainted with Original Sin. Judaism affirms life

    as good and seeks to endow it with spiritual and moral worth. The

    Jewish affirmation of faith emphasizes God's unity and is expressed in

    the Sh'ma: "Hear, O Israel, The Lord Our God, The Lord Is One."

ORTHODOX JUDAISM   Page 6

Literature, Ethics, Recruiting, Relationships

CREEDAL STATEMENTS AND/OR AUTHORITATIVE LITERATURE: Judaism is a religion

of deed rather than creed. The deeds required of a Jew are both ritual

and ethical, the former in relation to God and the latter in relation

to one's fellowman. Authoritative Jewish literature includes the

Bible, the Talmud, the Responsa literature, and the Codes. The most

authoritative Code is the Shulhan Arukh by Joseph Caro.

ETHICAL PRACTICES: Ethics is inseparable from religion in Judaism, and the

deepest concern of the Torah in its broadest sense is morality, both

individual and social.

HOW DOES ORTHODOX JUDAISM RECRUIT MEMBERS? Membership in Judaism is through

birth to a Jewish mother. In addition, although Judaism is not a

proselytizing religion, it does have procedures for conversion to

Judaism of those who freely and of their own accord seek to embrace it.

RELATIONSHIP WITH OTHER RELIGIONS: Throughout its venerable history, Judaism

has come in contact with many peoples, religions, and creeds. It has

both influenced and been influenced by these; yet it has ever retained

its religious and cultural uniqueness and has remained true to the

principles of ethical montheism. Judaism does not seek to supplant

other religions, but rather to labor with them in honorable fellowship

to bring about universal peace and justice on earth, and the light of

God to the hearts of all men.

RECONSTRUCTIONIST JUDAISM	Rabbi Ludwig Nadelmann,
Jewish Reconstructionist Foundation	Executive Vice President
432 Park Avenue, South	Rabbi Ira Eisenstein, President
New York, New York 10016	

HISTORICAL ROOTS: The history of Judaism is chronicled in the Bible and its

subsequent development is detailed in the vast, post-Biblical rabbinic

literature. Of the four major branches of Judaism, Reconstructionist

Judaism traces its beginnings to the 1920s when Mordecai Kaplan estab-

lished an experimental synagogue in New York City, the Society for the

Advancement of Judaism.

CURRENT WORLD LEADERS: No single world leader. Qualified rabbis join the

Reconstructionist Rabbinical Association; congregations, the Reconstruc-

tionist Federation of Congregations and Fellowships. The coordinating

body for Jewish Reconstructionist activity in the United States is the

Jewish Reconstructionist Foundation, headed by Rabbis Ira Eisenstein

and Ludwig Nadelman.

ORIGINS IN THE U.S.: Reconstructionist Judaism arose as a response to the

climate of naturalism and functionalism in American thought. It func-

tioned as a school of thought in the 1920s and 1930s. Professor Kaplan

served as a teacher of philosophy of religion at the Conservative

Jewish Theological Seminary in New York City and had great influence

over his disciples. In 1935, the bi-weekly Reconstructionist magazine

was launched, and in 1940, the Jewish Reconstructionist Foundation

was established to disseminate Reconstructionist ideology. This was

followed in 1951 by the establishment of the Reconstructionist Federa-

tion of Congregations and Fellowships of which individual local congre-

gations become a part. At present, the Federation has 36 affiliates in

the U.S. and Canada. In 1968, the Reconstructionist Rabbinical College

RECONSTRUCTIONIST JUDAISM	Page 2

Origins, Organization, Leaders, Worship

ORIGINS (continued): was established in Philadelphia (2308 N. Broad St.;
   19132) for the training of rabbis. The Reconstructionist Rabbinical
   Association came into being in 1973. Other national organizations affiliated with the Reconstructionist movement are a women's organization
   and a university fellowship.

NUMBER OF ADHERENTS IN THE U.S.: Approximately 50,000 of the more than
   5,000,000 Jews in the U.S. have some formal affiliation, either with a
   Reconstructionist congregation or as individuals. Reconstructionist
   Judaism is the only branch of Judaism with which families may affiliate
   as individuals in the absence of a Reconstructionist congregation.

ORGANIZATIONAL STRUCTURE: At the local level, the organizational unit is
   either a Reconstructionist synagogue or a small group, called Havurot,
   which meets for purposes of worship, study, and celebration. Each
   congregation is autonomous and elects its own rabbinical and lay
   leadership (see also "Current World Leaders").

LEADERSHIP AND ROLE OF RABBIS: The rabbi is the appointed spiritual leader
   who guides and represents the congregation. In addition, there are
   elected lay leaders, both in the congregation and in the larger Jewish
   community.

WHO MAY CONDUCT WORSHIP SERVICES? A rabbi, cantor, or any knowledgeable
   Jew (man or woman) may conduct worship services.

IS GROUP WORSHIP REQUIRED? Yes. Jewish worship is distinguished by its
   congregational or group character. Wherever possible, the traditional
   quorum of ten adults should be assembled for congregational worship.

RECONSTRUCTIONIST JUDAISM

Worship, Requirements

GROUP WORSHIP (continued): There are set times for daily, Sabbath and
   festival services, and Reconstructionist Jews are expected to attend
   and participate. In the absence of congregational worship
   services, every Jew can pray privately at this home or wherever he
   may be.

WORSHIP REQUIREMENTS: The requirement for private as well as public worship is that a Jew approach God with ethical integrity and that his
   prayers be guided by a spirit of sincerity and a readiness to identify with the Jewish people, its history, and tradition.

MINIMUM EQUIPMENT FOR PUBLIC WORSHIP: The Torah or the Scroll of the Law
   and its accouterments, prayer books, Hebrew Bible, skullcaps, and
   prayer shawls.

FACILITIES FOR WORSHIP: The facility for worship should be in keeping with
   the solemn dignity of the activity of prayer. Preferably it should be
   oriented to the East so that those worshiping within can pray facing
   the East. In addition, it should contain the ark which houses the Torah
   and adequate storage space for worship equipment.

OTHER SPECIFIC RELIGIOUS REQUIREMENTS OTHER THAN WORSHIP: Judaism requires
   that all aspects of life be sanctified. The relationship between man
   and his God is paralleled by the relationship between man and man.
   Jewish teaching is explicit in its insistence that human interrelation-
   ships are an expression and an experience of the divine in life.

DIETARY LAWS AND RESTRICTIONS: Observance of the Jewish dietary laws is
   encouraged. For Reconstructionist Jews, these are a matter of personal

RECONSTRUCTIONIST JUDAISM	Page 4

Requirements

DIET (continued): choice. The eating of Matzot (unleavened bread on Passover) is observed by most Reconstructionist Jews.

SPECIAL RELIGIOUS HOLIDAYS: In addition to the Sabbath, religious holidays
include the three Biblical Pilgrimage festivals - Pesach (Passover),
Shavuot (Pentecost), and Succot (Tabernacles) - and Rosh Hashannah
(New Year) and Yom Kippur (Day of Atonement). The first and last days
of Pesach and Succot, and the first day of Shavuot, are considered full
religious holidays. The festivals of Hanukkah and Purim and the fast
day of Tisha B'Av should be observed, but do not constitute full religious holidays.

FUNERAL AND BURIAL REQUIREMENTS: The purpose of Jewish funeral and burial
requirements is both to honor the deceased and to provide comfort to
the mourners. Observance of traditional practices is a matter of
personal choice, decided upon by the family in consultation with the
rabbi.

AUTOPSY: Reconstructionist Judaism does not object to autopsy, and certainly approves of it when it involves health considerations or pro-
motes the ends of justice.

CREMATION: Individual choice. In belief and practice, most Reconstructionist Jews choose burial in the ground, in keeping with Jewish custom.

MEDICAL TREATMENT: No restrictions. Jews believe that maintaining good
health is both an individual obligation and a group responsibility, and
medical treatment is one means to help achieve good health.

RECONSTRUCTIONIST JUDAISM	Page 5
Requirements, Position on Service, Beliefs	

UNIFORM OR APPEARANCE REQUIREMENTS: Reconstructionist Jews have no uniform

or appearance requirements except for the use of the prayer shawl

(Talit) at public morning services. Reconstructionist Jews also cover

their heads when engaged in prayer.

POSITION ON SERVICE IN ARMED FORCES: Jews have served in the military in

all U.S. wars, to defend their country and to help to maintain it free

and strong. Judaism also allows for an individual Jew to conscien-

tiously object to service in the military.

IS A RABBI REQUIRED AT THE TIME OF DEATH? Anyone in the presence of a dying

person may guide him in the expression of Vidui (confession) and the

affirmation of faith (the Sh'ma), but the presence of a rabbi is im-

portant both for guidance and consolation.

ANY OTHER PRACTICES OR TEACHINGS WHICH MAY CONFLICT WITH MILITARY DIRECTIVES

OR PRACTICES: While the basic philosophy of Judaism is the sanctifica-

tion of life, it recognizes the necessity to preserve and defend one's

country, without which the "sanctification of life" becomes a meaning-

less phrase.

BASIC TEACHINGS OR BELIEFS: Reconstructionism defines Judaism as the evolv-

ing religious civilization of the Jewish people. The religious values

and culture of Judaism are the outgrowth of the historical experience

of the Jews. The idea of God is rooted in human experience and has

gone through various stages of development and continues to do so. The

Sacred Scriptures reveal the search of the Jewish people, its leaders

and prophets, for the meaning of God in human life. Man is free, and

RECONSTRUCTIONIST JUDAISM	Page 6
Beliefs, Literature, Ethics, Recruiting, Relationship	

BASIC TEACHINGS OR BELIEFS (continued): there is no doctrine of original

sin in Reconstructionist Judaism. Together with other groups in

Judaism, they affirm that man is good. The Jewish affirmation "Hear

O Israel, the Lord Our God, The Lord Is One" is a statement of faith

in the basic unity of all existence.

CREEDAL STATEMENTS AND/OR AUTHORITATIVE LITERATURE: Central to Judaism is

the deed, and the Jewish concept of the Mitzvah consists in the perfor-

mance of acts which attest to the sanctity of life. Sacred Jewish lit-

erature, includes the Bible, the Talmad, the Responsa literature, the

Codes, and the Siddui (prayer book). The prayer book is not a closed

book and goes through periodic changes reflecting recent historical

experience and new ethical insights.

ETHICAL PRACTICES: Ethics is an integral part of Judaism and affects every

aspect of Jewish life. Ritual alone does not exhaust Jewish lifestyle.

HOW DOES JUDAISM RECRUIT MEMBERS? Membership in Judaism primarily is through

birth. In addition, although Judaism is not a *proselytizing* religion,

it does have procedures for conversion of those who freely and of their

own accord seek to embrace it.

RELATIONSHIP TO OTHER RELIGIONS: Throughout its history, Judaism has come

in contact with many peoples, religions, and creeds. It has both in-

fluenced and been influenced by these; yet it has always retained its

religious and cultural distinctiveness. Judaism does not seek to sup-

plant other religions, but rather to labor with them in fellowship to

bring about universal peace and justice on earth.

REFORM JUDAISM   Rabbi Malcolm H. Stern
Central Conference of American Rabbis
790 Madison Avenue
New York, New York   10021

HISTORICAL ROOTS: Judaism's history is chronicled in the Bible, and subse-
    quently detailed in post-Biblical rabbinic literature. Of the three
    major branches of Judaism today, Reform Judaism, which began as a result
    of Jewish Emancipation in 19th century Germany and the subsequent break-
    down of the Ghetto walls, attempts to meet the demands of modern life by
    introducing modifications in traditional Jewish thought and practice.

CURRENT WORLD LEADERS: No single world leader. Qualified rabbis identify
    with Reform Judaism by joining the Central Conference of American Rabbis.
    Congregations identify themselves as Reform by joining the Union of
    American Hebrew Congregations (see also "Organizational Structure)".

ORIGINS IN THE U.S.: In 1824, 47 members of Congregation Beth Elohim in
    Charleston, SC, requested reforms in the ritual and the introduction of
    English prayers in the worship service. When the congregation rejected
    the request, a group of members withdrew and founded a new congregation
    on November 21, 1824, and named it "The Reformed Society of Israelites."
    While this congregation did not last, its example led to the creation of
    others, such as Har Sinai in Baltimore and Emanu-El in New York.

        Rabbi Isaac Mayer Wise of Cincinnati, in 1873, succeeded in uniting
    a group of congregations to create the Union of American Hebrew Congre-
    gations (UAHC) (see also "Organizational Structure").

NUMBER OF ADHERENTS IN THE U.S.: Approximately 1,200,000 of the more than
    5,000,000 Jews in the U.S. have some formal affiliation with a Reform
    congregation.

REFORM JUDAISM	Page 2
Organization, Leaders, Worship	

ORGANIZATIONAL STRUCTURE: Reform Jewish Congregations are self-governing religious communities, each of which elects its own rabbinic and lay leadership. Approximately 715 congregations are currently members of the Union of American Hebrew Congregations (UAHC). Other national organizations, offshoots of UAHC, are the National Federation of Temple Sisterhoods, the National Federations of Temple Brotherhoods, the National Federation of Temple Youth, the American Conference of Cantors, and the National Associations of both Temple Educators and Administrators. In 1875, UAHC created a training school for American Reform Rabbis, the Hebrew Union College of Cincinnati, which now includes campuses in New York, Los Angeles, and Jerusalem, Israel.

LEADERSHIP AND ROLE OF THE RABBIS: The rabbi is the trained spiritual leader selected by the congregation to guide and represent the congregation. In addition, there are elected lay leaders, both in the Congregation and in the larger Jewish community.

WHO MAY CONDUCT WORSHIP SERVICES? Usually a rabbi, often assisted by a cantor, with active participation by congregants. Any knowledgeable Jew may conduct worship services in the absence of a rabbi.

IS A GROUP WORSHIP REQUIRED? Yes. Jewish worship is distinguished by its congregational or group nature. There are set times for congregational worship and Reform Jews are expected to attend and participate in these.

WORSHIP REQUIREMENTS: Reform Judaism has published prayer books for public worship. Jews are also encouraged to have many home ceremonials in connection with the Sabbath and festivals, and to pray daily. Home

REFORM JUDAISM	Page 3
Worship, Requirements	

WORSHIP REQUIREMENTS (continued): prayer books have been published for use in home ceremonials and individual prayers.

MINIMUM EQUIPMENT FOR WORSHIP: Public worship requires the Torah, or Scroll of the Law and its accouterments, prayer books, and Hebrew Bible. Skull-caps and prayer-shawls are optional.

FACILITIES FOR WORSHIP: A synagogue, usually oriented to the East so that worshipers can pray facing Jerusalem. Every synagogue contains the ark which houses the Torah and adequate storage space for worship equipment.

OTHER SPECIFIC RELIGIOUS REQUIREMENTS OTHER THAN WORSHIP: Judaism requires that all aspects of life be sanctified. Since the vertical relationship between man and God is paralleled by a horizontal relationship between man and man, Reform Judaism lays special emphasis on ethical social behavior and follows the teaching of Israel's prophets in upholding social justice for all.

DIETARY LAWS AND RESTRICTIONS: A matter of personal choice.

SPECIAL RELIGIOUS HOLIDAYS: In addition to upholding and observing the Sabbath, Reform Judaism celebrates three Biblical Pilgrimage festivals, Pesah (Passover - March or April), Shavuot (Pentecost - May or June), and Succot (Tabernacles - September or October), as well as Hanukkah (Feast of Lights - November or December) and Purim (Feast of Esther - February or March). Major emphasis is placed on observing Rosh Hashanah (New Year) and Yom Kippur (Day of Atonement), both in September or October. Most Reform congregations observe Rosh Hashanah for one day, in keeping with the Bible.

REFORM JUDAISM	Page 4

Requirements, Position on Service

FUNERAL AND BURIAL REQUIREMENTS: The purpose of Jewish funeral and burial requirements is both to honor the deceased and to provide comfort to the mourners. Observance of traditional practices is a matter of personal choice, decided upon by the family in consultation with a rabbi.

AUTOPSY: Permitted when medically necessary, unless the family objects.

CREMATION: Individual choice. Most choose burial in the earth.

MEDICAL TREATMENT: No restrictions. Acceptance and use of the latest medical advances for physical and mental health are encouraged.

UNIFORM APPEARANCE REQUIREMENTS: Generally no distinctive garb. Rabbis and congregants may opt for special accouterments at worship, such as robes for use at the pulpit, head covering, and prayer shawls.

POSITION ON SERVICE IN THE ARMED FORCES: Jews have served in the military in all U.S. wars, to defend their country and to help maintain it free and strong. However, Judaism also upholds the right of any individual to object conscientiously to serve in the military.

IS A RABBI REQUIRED AT THE TIME OF DEATH? Anyone in the presence of a dying person may guide them in the expression of Vidui (confession) and the affirmation of faith (the Sh'ma), but the presence of a rabbi is valuable both for guidance and consolation.

ANY OTHER PRACTICES OR TEACHINGS WHICH MAY CONFLICT WITH MILITARY DIRECTIVES OR PRACTICE: While the basic philosophy of Judaism is the sanctification of life, it recognizes the necessity to preserve and defend one's country, without which the "sanctification of life" becomes a meaningless phrase.

| REFORM JUDAISM | Page 5 |

Beliefs, Literature, Ethics

BASIC TEACHINGS OR BELIEFS: Judaism is a religion based on *progressive revelation*. Reform Judaism believes that the Bible describes their ancestors' search for the nature of God and His requirements of human beings. Developing human knowledge has brought further revelation of God's omnipresence (present in all places at all times), omnipotence (unlimited power), and omniscience (unlimited knowledge and insight). Prayer is our way of communicating with Him directly without any intercessor. For Jews, every soul is born with capacity for good and evil, but Judaism affirms life as good and seeks to endow it with spiritual and moral worth. Immortality of the soul is the inheritance of everyone, especially those who are remembered for good.

CREEDAL STATEMENTS AND/OR AUTHORITATIVE LITERATURE: Judaism "is a religion of deed, rather than creed" (see also "Ethical Practices"). However, all Jews subscribe to the Unity of God as expressed in the Sh'ma: "Hear, O Israel, the Lord our God, the Lord is One." Reform Judaism bases its teachings primarily on the Bible (commonly referred to as the "Old Testament" by Christians and others). However, in recent years, it has developed a literature of optional rituals (see also "Worship Requirements").

ETHICAL PRACTICES: (See also "Other Specific Religious Requirements Other Than Worship".) The deeds required of a Jew are both ritual and ethical; the former in relation to God, and the latter in relation to one's fellowman. Reform Judaism emphasizes ethical social behavior and social justice for all.

REFORM JUDAISM   Page 6

Recruiting, Relationships

HOW DOES REFORM JUDAISM RECRUIT MEMBERS? Membership in Judaism is primarily

   through birth. In addition, although Judaism is not a *proselytizing*

   religion, it does have procedures for conversion to Judaism of those who

   freely and of their own accord seek to embrace it. Reform Judaism

   actively encourages willing converts, and has programs for training them.

RELATIONSHIP TO OTHER RELIGIONS: Reform Judaism is one of the three major

   branches of Judaism today. Throughout its history, Judaism has come in

   contact with many peoples, religions, and creeds. It has both influenced

   them and been influenced by them; yet it retains its religious and cul-

   tural uniqueness and remains true to the basic principles of ethical

   monotheism which are its basic teachings. Judaism does not seek to sup-

   plant other religions, but rather to labor with them in fellowship to

   bring about universal peace and justice on earth, and the light of God

   to all of mankind.

INTRODUCTION: SIKH GROUPS

The early 16th century was a time of bitter conflict in North India. A series of invasions which culminated in 1526 established Muslim supremacy. The Punjab area was one of the most hotly contested regions, and it was here that Nanak (1469-1539) was born. One day while bathing in a river, he had a vision of God's presence in which he was told to go into the world and teach the repetition of the Name of God, the practice of charity, meditation and worship, and the keeping of ritual purity through absolution.

According to tradition, after a full day of silence, he uttered the pronouncement, "There is no Hindu (the native faith of India) and no Musselman (Muslim)." He adopted a unique garb which combined both Hindu and Muslim features, and developed an *eclectic* faith which took elements from many religions, principally Hindus and Muslims. From Islam he taught of One Creator God, called the True Name to avoid such designations as Allah or Vishnu. From Hinduism he taught the ideas of karma, reincarnation and the ultimate unreality of the world. Nanak also emphasized the unique role of the guru (teacher) as necessary to lead people to God. After Nanak's death, nine gurus followed him in succession.

The fourth guru, Ram Dass, began the Golden Temple of Amritsar, the present headquarters of the world Sikh community. The fifth guru, Arjan, completed the Temple and installed the <u>Siri Guru Granth Sahib</u>, or <u>Adi Granth</u>, the collected writings of Nanak, within it.

The tenth guru Gobind Singh (1666-1718) had the most significant role in molding the Sikh community other than Nanak. He completed the <u>Adi Granth</u> in its present form and militarized the Sikhs by forming the Khalsa, the Community

of the Pure. Members were initiated by baptism in which they drank and were
sprinkled with sweetened water stirred with a sword. They changed their name
to Singh (Lion) and adopted the five Ks: (1) Kesh, or long hair, a sign of
saintliness; (2) Kangh, a comb for keeping the hair neat; (3) Kach, short pants
for quick movement in battle; (4) Kara, a steel bracelet signifying sternness
and restraint; (5) Kirpan, a sword of defense.

After Gobind Singh's death, the Adi Granth became the guru and no further
human guru's were allowed. The military emphasis continued, however, and the
Sikhs served with distinction in British army units.

In the 19th century, variant forms of Sikhism emerged. Param Guru Shri
Shiv Dayal Singh Sahib began to gather followers, and in 1861 formed the
Radhasoami Satsang. It was distinguished from other forms of Sikhism by the
development of a new line of gurus. Both the Radhasoami Satsang and the Ruhani
Satsang, which came from it, have been transplanted to the United States. The
Sikh Dharma and its education branch, the Healthy, Happy, Holy Organization,
represent orthodox Sikhism.

HEALTH, HAPPY, HOLY ORGANIZATION 3HO Foundation 1620 Preliss Road Los Angeles, California 90036	Yogi Bhajan (Siri Singh Sahib Harbhajan Singh Khalsa Yogiji)

HISTORICAL ROOTS: The 3HO Foundation was started in 1969 in Los Angeles as a non-profit, religious, and educational organization dedicated to making available the techniques of Kundalini Yoga and meditation as tools for the improvement of the quality of life. Siri Sing Sahib Harbhajan Singh Khalsa Yogiji, also known as Yogi Bhajan, has served as Spiritual Director of 3HO since its beginning. The 3HO Foundation has rapidly expanded since its inception, and presently is represented by over 110 teaching centers worldwide. All of the teachers in 3HO are also ministers of the Sikh Dharma, and hence the organization has become de facto the educational branch of Sikh Dharma, although no formal connection exists. (Many members of 3HO are not Sikhs.)

CURRENT WORLD LEADER: Siri Singh Sahib Harbhajan Singh Khalsa Yogiji (also known as Yogi Bhajan).

ORIGINS IN U.S.: Yogi Bhajan emigrated from India to Toronto in 1968, and moved later that same year to Los Angeles where he started an ashram, or teacher training center (see also "Historical Roots").

NUMBER OF MEMBERS IN U.S.: Approximately 250,000. Of these, approximately 5,000 reside in ashrams.

ORGANIZATIONAL STRUCTURE: The 3HO Foundation is incorporated separately in each state in which it maintains an ashram, or teaching center. The local ashrams are run by an Ashram Director who is appointed by the Siri Singh Sahib. The Siri Singh Sahib is overall spiritual director for all branches of 3HO.

HEALTH, HAPPY, HOLY ORGANIZATION	Page 2
Leadership, Worship, Requirements, Position on Service	

LEADERSHIP AND ROLE OF ASHRAM DIRECTORS: Directors of 3HO ashrams are

    charged with administering the communal affairs of the members.

WHO MAY CONDUCT CLASSES? Qualified teachers conduct the various class of-

    ferings, which include yoga, nutrition, and other subjects (see also

    "Basic Teachings").

IS GROUP WORSHIP REQUIRED? Communal meditation is practiced by members in

    ashrams.

WORSHIP REQUIREMENTS: None applicable.

FACILITIES FOR WORSHIP: Ashrams are used by members for their meditation.

OTHER SPECIFIC RELIGIOUS REQUIREMENTS OTHER THAN WORSHIP: None applicable.

DIETARY LAWS OR RESTRICTIONS: Vegetarian.

SPECIAL RELIGIOUS HOLIDAYS: None.

FUNERAL AND BURIAL REQUIREMENTS: None.

AUTOPSY: None.

MEDICAL TREATMENT: None.

UNIFORM APPEARANCES: No requirements, except among members who are prac-

    ticing Sikhs.

POSITION ON SERVICE IN THE ARMED FORCES: None.

IS A TEACHER REQUIRED AT THE TIME OF DEATH? No.

ANY OTHER PRACTICES OR TEACHINGS WHICH MAY CONFLICT WITH MILITARY DIRECTIVES

    OR PRACTICE: None.

BASIC TEACHINGS OR BELIEFS: The 3HO Foundation maintains teaching centers

    for the purpose of offering classes to the general public in Kundalini

    Yoga (a technique which releases untapped human energy), meditation

HEALTH, HAPPY, HOLY ORGANIZATION	Page 3
Basic Beliefs, Literature, Ethics, Recruiting, Relationships	

BASIC TEACHINGS OR BELIEFS (continued): (a means of understanding oneself,

leading to realization of human potential), natural foods cooking,

nutrition, and other subjects aimed at improving the quality of life.

CREEDAL STATEMENTS AND/OR AUTHORITATIVE LITERATURE: None (except insofar

as members who are devotees of Sikh Dharma are concerned). Sikhs

believe that their way of life is but one of many paths to God: by

extension 3HO, as the educational arm of Sikh Dharma, can be con-

sidered open to members of all faiths. Literature includes: A)

The Teachings of Yogi Bhajan, Hawthorne Press; B) Kundalini Quar-

terly, KRI Press (Pomona, California); C) Beads of Truth, 3HO

International, 1620 Preliss Road, Los Angeles, California.

ETHICAL PRACTICES: No requirements.

HOW DOES 3HO RECRUIT: 3HO advertises its various class offerings by means

of posters, booklets, etc., in order to attract participants.

RELATIONSHIP WITH OTHER GROUPS: 3HO maintains open channels of communi-

cation with educational, spiritual, and civic bodies.

SIKH DHARMA
International Headquarters
1620 Preuss Road
Los Angeles, California 90036

Singh Sahib Harbhajan
Singh Khalsa Yogiji
(Yogi Bhajan)

HISTORICAL ROOTS: The Sikh Dharma was founded in the 16th century as a reform movement; it drew from the universal aspects of many religions,
especially Hinduism and Islam. The founder was Guru Nanak (1469-1538),
who was followed by a succession of nine other gurus, or teachers, who
laid a firm foundation for the spiritual, social, and political community
of Sikhs. Guru Arjun, the fifth Guru, compiled the writings and hymns
of his predecessors into a volume of scriptures which was completed and
put into its present form by Guru Gobind Singh, the tenth master. This
volume, the Siri Guru Granth Sahib, is now recognized as the only living
embodiment of the spirit of Guru Nanak and is held in highest reverence
by all Sikhs.

CURRENT WORLD LEADER: The S.G.P.C., located at the Golden Temple, in Amritsar, India, is recognized as the chief administrative body of the Sikh
Dharma, while the Akal Takt (same location) is revered as the supreme
spiritual authority. In 1971, Siri Singh Sahib Harbhajan Khalsa Yogiji
(also known as Yogi Bhajan) was ordained by the Akal Takt to be both
spiritual and administrative leader for the Sikh Dharma in all parts of
the world outside of India.

ORIGINS IN THE U.S.: Although Sikh Dharma began in India, Sikhs immigrated
to the U.S. beginning in the 19th century. In 1969, the Siri Singh Sahib (Yogi Bhajan) brought the teachings of the Sikh way of life to large
numbers of Americans. Since that time, the religion has spread rapidly,
so that today over 150 congregations of Sikhs exist in the western world.

SIKH DHARMA   Page 2

Organization, Leadership, Worship

NUMBER OF ADHERENTS IN THE U.S.: There are approximately 300,000 Sikhs in
     the United States, directly or indirectly affiliated with the more than
     150 congregations (see "Origins in the U.S.").

ORGANIZATIONAL STRUCTURE: The organization of Sikh Dharma in the West is con-
     ceived of as an inverse pyramid; each level, starting with the Siri Singh
     Sahib at the bottom supports and serves the level(s) above it. Above the
     Siri Singh Sahib is the Khalsa Council made up of the Mukhia Singh Sahibs
     (male regional ministers) and Mukhia Sardarni Sahiba (female regional
     ministers), as well as other ministers appointed by the Siri Singh Sahib.
     The Khalsa Council meets quarterly and is headed the Secretary General,
     presently Mukhia Sardarni Sahiba Sardarni Premka Kaur Khalsa. The re-
     gional ministers function as liaisons between the Council and local con-
     gregations, each led by local ministers (a Singh Sahib or a Sardarni
     Sahiba).

LEADERSHIP AND ROLE OF MINISTERS: Each local congregation is led by a minis-
     ter, who is trained as a teacher and authorized by the Siri Singh Sahib
     to administer to the needs of all those who practice the Sikh way of life.

WHO MAY CONDUCT WORSHIP SERVICES? Anyone.

IS GROUP WORSHIP REQUIRED? No, but it is stressed, as development of "group
     consciousness" is basic to Sikh Dharma. Daily worship at a Gurdwara
     (literally, "gate of the guru" or temple) is recommended.

WORSHIP REQUIREMENTS: Each Sikh is enjoined to practice his or her Sadhana
     (Spiritual Discipline). This Sadhana consists of reciting the "Banis" or

SIKH DHARMA   Page 3

Worship, Requirements

WORSHIP REQUIREMENTS (continued): Sikh prayers, meditation, and the chanting

of God's Name for at least an hour.

MINIMUM EQUIPMENT FOR WORSHIP: Sikhs should maintain a copy of the "Nit Nem"

or daily prayers of the Sikh Dharma. Optional literature would include

the "Peace Lagoon" and other translations of the Sikh Scriptures.

FACILITIES FOR WORSHIP: None required, although Sikhs traditionally worship

together at a Gurdwara.

OTHER SPECIFIC RELIGIOUS REQUIREMENTS OTHER THAN WORSHIP: A Sikh has certain

symbols (see "Uniform Appearance Requirements") which he or she is di-

rected to wear as a reminder of religious principles.

DIETARY LAWS OR RESTRICTIONS: The Scriptures specifically prohibit the eating

of fish and meat, and the consumption of alcohol or any other intoxicant

or drug.

SPECIAL RELIGIOUS HOLIDAYS: Traditional holidays of the Sikh Dharma are

Baisakhi Day (in April) - the birthday of the Khalsa; the Martyrdom Days

of Guru Tegh Bhadur (in November) and Guru Arjun Dev (in May); and the

birthdays of all ten of the Sikh Gurus, especially Guru Nanak (ca.

November 25), Guru Ram Dass (ca. October 29), and Guru Gobind Singh (ca.

December 22).

FUNERAL AND BURIAL REQUIREMENTS: Sikhs are traditionally cremated. Normally

the body should be prepared for cremation by a qualified minister.

AUTOPSY: No restrictions.

CREMATION: Preferred.

SIKH DHARMA	Page 4

Requirements, Position on Service, Basic Beliefs

MEDICAL TREATMENT: Sikhs prefer natural methods of preventative medicine and
  healing, i.e., exercise, nourishing food, etc. In severe cases allo-
  pathic procedures and/or surgery are acceptable.

UNIFORM APPEARANCE REQUIREMENTS: All Sikhs are directed by the order of Guru
  Gobind Singh to keep all their hair uncut (including beards) and to keep
  their hair tied on the top of the head in a turban. Uncut hair, known as
  kesh, is kept neat by a kangha, or comb. Sikhs also wear kachera, a special underwear originally designed to allow freedom of movement in battle;
  the kara, a steel bracelet which is a sign of an inseparable bond with
  God; and the kirpan, a dagger which represents the commitment of Sikhs to
  defend truth, righteousness, and those who cannot defend themselves.
  Ministers of the Sikh Dharma normally wear special dress: a long hemmed
  skirt (kurta) and chudidas, which are a special kind of pants that are
  tight around the lower legs and loose at the waist (very similar to
  jodhpurs).

POSITION ON SERVICE IN THE ARMED FORCES: Sikhs have traditionally been outstanding soliders, beginning with their own community's battles with
  local suppressive forces, and later as members of the British and Indian
  armies. They stress patriotism, freedom, and commitment to one's country.

IS A MINISTER REQUIRED AT TIME OF DEATH? No, but required for the cremation
  ritual.

ANY OTHER PRACTICES OR TEACHINGS WHICH MAY CONFLICT WITH MILITARY DIRECTIVES
  OR PRACTIC: None, except the appearance requirements.

Basic Beliefs, Literature, Ethics

BASIC TEACHINGS OR BELIEFS: Sikh Dharma teaches that there is one God who

   created all beings. He is the One upon whom we all depend for our next

   breath and hence for our life. He is Self-existent, Immortal, Immanent,

   Transcendent, Omnipotent, Omnipresent, and Omniscient. God is experi-

   ence through "Nam," meditation on the primal creative sound current

   which gives life to all creation.

        According to Guru Nanak, a Sikh should constantly praise the One

   Creator. This praise is given by chanting the Name of God, which in the

   original language is "Sat Nam" (God's name is Truth) or "Wahe Guru"

   (Experience of Infinite Wisdom). Chanting God's name is also done by

   repeating the mantra, "Ek Ong Kar Sat Nam Siri Wha Guru," which trans-

   lates, "There is one Creator and one creation, Truth is His name. He is

   all Great, He is all Wisdom."

CREEDAL STATEMENTS AND/OR AUTHORITATIVE LITERATURE: The Siri Guru Granth

   Sahib, the living embodiment of the guru, is the supreme authority among

   all Sikhs. Peace Lagoon, an English translation of parts of the Granth,

   is widely used among English-speaking Sikhs. Also recommended is Guru

   for the Aquarian Age by Sardarni Premka Kaur. The Sikh Rehit Maryada is

   a written code of ethics and protocol which all Sikhs are directed to

   obey.

ETHICAL PRACTICES: The Sikh lifestyle is centered on the idea of the spirit-

   ual family, which may be achieved in community life. Members are direc-

   ted to rise before sunrise and chant God's name and meditate, work by the

SIKH DHARMA   Page 6

Ethics, Recruiting, Relationships

ETHICAL PRACTICES (continued): sweat of their brow, share with others, and
    live righteously (put the need of others first). Sikhs are encouraged
    to learn "Gurmukhi," the language in which the scriptures are written.

HOW DOES SIKH DHARMA RECRUIT MEMBERS? The Sikh Dharma is a non-*proselytizing*
    way of life, and new members are not recruited. However, people seeing
    the example of righteous living set by Sikhs often inquire, investigate
    and adopt the Sikh way of life as their own. The Sikh Dharma publishes
    periodicals, e.g., Sikh Dharma Magazine, as well as other materials.
    Initiation into Sikh Dharma is not necessary, but a Sikh can join the
    Khalsa - "pure ones" - by a formal baptism initiated by Guru Gobind
    Singh; as a result of this baptism, the "pure one" must live a total and
    unswerving commitment to the principles of the Dharma.

RELATIONSHIP WITH OTHER RELIGIONS: The Golden Temple at Amritsar has four
    sides, each with a door, symbolic that Sikh Dharma is open to all people
    of all religions. It is one of many paths to God. A Sikh is merely a
    seeker of truth.

INTRODUCTION: OTHER GROUPS

The groups considered in this section manifest the wide variety of religious options available in the U.S. They draw upon several distinct religious impulses, each with a long heritage.

PSYCHIC GROUPS

From ancient times, people have claimed powers of mind and spirit far surpassing those recognized by modern science. In years past, these phenomena (e.g., spiritual healing, telepathy, clairvoyance, mind over matter) were termed "supernatural"; they are now known as "psychic," and studied by scientists.

The contemporary psychic growth began in the 1700s with the work of such people as Swedenborg and Mesmer. In the 1800s, Spiritualism, with a strong belief in mediumship (the ability of some people to enter a trance-like state and contact spirits of the departed), emerged and spread. Partially in reaction to Spiritualism, Madame Blavatsky founded the Theosophical Society in 1875, to promote universal brotherhood, the study of religion and psychology, and the investigation of the mystic powers of man and nature.

The growth of psychic practitioners led to the development of psychical research. The British Society for Psychical Research was established in 1880, and the American Society in 1882. In studying psychic phenomena, Dr. Rhinehas of Duke University coined the term "extra-sensory perception (ESP)" and helped make "parapsychology" a discipline of study. The growth of parapsychology, including its membership in the American Association for the Advancement of Science, provided a dynamic base upon which psychic groups could build.

Psychic religious groups, including the Church of Scientology and the Foundation Faith of the Millenium, have a wide belief span. In general, they believe in the reality of the phenomena studied by parapsychologists. They usually offer members various ways to develop their powers, and some have members with special abilities which can be used by individuals to aid in dealing with personal problems.

There are several hundred psychically-oriented bodies in the U.S. The two considered here grow out of this general background, and are not directly related to other bodies.

MAGICK

Magick (not "magic," which is considered a stage performer's art and not a religion) groups have experienced considerable growth since the 1960s. These groups are distinguished by their use of occult practices (astrology and divination) and magick (the ability to willfully change the world by manipulating the cosmic forces). While like the psychic dimension, magick is as old as known history. Its contemporary revival, however, began in the early 1900s.

The most popular form of magick is witchcraft. Not to be confused with Satanism, witchcraft is a nature-oriented religion based on the worship of the male-female polarity, the observance of the agricultural seasons, and magick. Worship of the male-female aspects of nature usually is expressed as allegiance to the Horned God and the Great Mother Goddess. Ritual follows the movement of the sun and moon.

Magick seeks mastery of all the cosmic forces believed to control the world. Witches believe in the ancient principle of "as above, so below," and in their worship seek to create a microcosm, a magical image of the whole. The universe is generally viewed as a sphere. The magical circle, drawn at the

beginning of all magical rituals, is the outline of the microcosm intersec-

ting the floor.

Witchcraft had grown slowly until the repeal of the last of England's

anti-witchcraft laws in the 1950s. Growth accelerated in the 1960s and

1970s. There are no less than thirty different witch (or the preferred

term "Wicca") groups plus numerous independent covens functioning in the

U.S. The American Council of Witches represents the traditionalist covens

which trace their ancestry to various medieval European traditions. The

Gardnerians are one of several modern Wicca groups. Others are the Alex-

andrians, the Algard, and the Church of Wicca of Bakersfield (CA). There

are also several miscellaneous traditions.

Secrecy is a major element of the existence of both witchcraft and

Satanism (discussed below). Secrecy is protective (known members often

lose their jobs, friends or status), and serves to guard the sacred myste-

ries of the group.

SATANISM

Often confused with witchcraft, Satanism is the worship of Satan (also

known as Baphomet or Lucifer). Classical Satanism, often involving "black

masses," human sacrifice, and other sacrilegious or illegal acts, is now

rare. Modern Satanism is based on both the knowledge of ritual magick and

the "anti-establishment" mood of the 1960s. It is related to classical

Satanism more in image than substance, and generally focuses on "rational

self-interest with ritualistic trappings."

The Church of Satan, begun by Anton LeVey, has spawned several similar groups, such as the Church of Satanic Brotherhood, the Ordo Templi Satanas, and the Congregation of Set.

INDIVIDUALLY DISTINCTIVE GROUPS

Within the variety of American religion are a number of groups which are highly individual in nature. That is, while their origins can often be traced to any number of the major world religions, they have developed beliefs, systems, or structures which are considerably different from those traditions.

Three of the groups discussed in this section fall within this general framework: the Baha'i World Fellowship, the Native American Church, and the Universal Life Church.

Baha'i is a major new faith built on the revelations given to several Persian mystics of the 19th century. While growing on an Islamic base, it has moved to a more universal outlook.

The Native American Church is one of many that uses psychedelic substances as a visionary aid and sacramental element. They are distinctive in being both the oldest and the only one with government sanction to use the designated drugs.

The Universal Life Church represents a response to the religious freedom in America by individuals with a strong independent strain in their religious thought.

The Universal Life Church has spawned over ten similar church bodies including the Crown of Life Fellowship, the Life Science Church, The Calvary Grace Church and the Brotherhood of Peace and Tranquility.

AMERICAN COUNCIL OF WITCHES c/o Mr. Carl L. Weschcke Llewellyn Publications 213 East 4th Street St. Paul, Minnesota 55101	Mr. Carl L. Weschcke AKA: Witches, Traditional Witchcraft, Wicca

HISTORICAL ROOTS: Witchcraft is the ancient *Pagan* faith of Pre-Christian Europe. This nature-oriented, agricultural, magical religion had no central organization, but was passed through families. During the Christian Era, particularly after the beginning of the systematic persecution of Witches in 1484, almost all public expressions of the Craft disappeared. Surviving in hidden and isolated places, Witchcraft has made a comeback in the Twentieth Century, partially spurred by the repeal of the last of the British Witchcraft Laws in 1951.

CURRENT WORLD LEADERSHIP: No central authority. Many Witches have, however, affiliated with the American Council of Witches, formed in 1974, to provide a structure for cooperation and mutual sharing.

ORIGINS IN THE U.S.: Brought to the U.S. in the 17th century by emigrants from Europe. Since then, many Witches from many ethnic and national traditions have brought their religious practices to the New World. It survived in the isolation of rural settings and the anonymity in the city. The 1960s saw a significant revival of the Craft, and many Witches and "covens" (local groups) became at least partially public. Many discovered others of like mind through the emerging *Pagan* press. A meeting in Minneapolis formed the American Council of Witches (1974) and a statement entitled "Principles of Wiccan Beliefs" was adopted.

NUMBER OF ADHERENTS IN THE U.S.: Unknown: between 10,000 and 100,000.

ORGANIZATIONAL STRUCTURE: The basic structure is the coven (local group) with 5 to 50 members (ideally 12-15) led by a High Priestess or High Priest.

AMERICAN COUNCIL OF WITCHES	Page 2

Organization, Leadership, Worship

ORGANIZATION (continued): The Priest and/or Priestess derives authority from

   initiation by another Witch. Some covens are tied together in fraternal

   relationships and acknowledge authority of a Priestess or Priest from

   whom orders are derived. Many are totally autonomous.

LEADERSHIP AND ROLE OF PRIESTESS AND/OR PRIEST: The High Priestess and/or

   High Priest has authority for the coven. Witches pass through three de-

   grees as they practice the Craft: (1) acknowledges one as a full member

   of the coven and initiates the process of mastering the skills of a

   Witch; (2) recognizes growth in ability and admits one to all the inner

   secrets; and (3) admits one to the priesthood.

WHO MAY CONDUCT WORSHIP SERVICES? A High Priestess or Priest.

IS GROUP WORSHIP REQUIRED? No, but it is encouraged.

WORSHIP REQUIREMENTS: None, but Witches are expected to practice their faith,

   which includes mastering magick, ritual, and psychic development and the

   regular worship of the Wiccan deities.

MINIMUM EQUIPMENT FOR WORSHIP: The "atheme," or ritual knife; the "pentacle,"

   a metal disc inscribed with magical symbols; a *chalice*; and a sword.

   Various traditions will demand other items.

FACILITIES FOR WORSHIP: Witches worship within a magick circle that is in-

   scribed on the ground or floor. The circle should be located so as to

   insure the privacy of the rituals.

OTHER SPECIFIC RELIGIOUS REQUIREMENTS OTHER THAN WORSHIP (see above): None.

DIETARY LAWS OR RESTRICTIONS: None.

AMERICAN COUNCIL OF WITCHES   Page 3

Holidays, Requirements, Position on Service

SPECIAL RELIGIOUS HOLIDAYS: The four great festivals are seasonal: (1)

   Spring *Equinox*. March 21; (2) Summer *Solstice* or Midsummer, June 22; (3)

   Autumn *Equinox*, September 21; and (4) Yule or Winter *Solstice*, December

   22. These are joined by four cross festivals related to the agricultural

   and herd-raising year: (1) Candlemas, February 2; (2) May Eve or Bel-

   tane, April 30; (3) Lammas, July 31; and (4) Halloween, October 31. Be-

   sides these eight, most Wicca groups meet either weekly or bi-weekly (on

   the full and new moon). Major holidays are termed sabbats, and weekly

   or bi-weekly meeting are esbats.

FUNERAL AND BURIAL REQUIREMENTS: Practices vary widely. In case of death,

   the coven to which the Witch belongs should be contacted.

AUTOPSY: Generally no restrictions.

CREMATION: Many prefer it, but local coven should be consulted.

MEDICAL TREATMENT: No restrictions.

UNIFORM APPEARANCE REQUIREMENTS: None are prescribed.

POSITION ON SERVICE IN THE ARMED FORCES: No official stance. Many Witches

   are presently military personnel, while others are conscientious objec-

   tors, derived from the generally pro-life stance of Wicca.

IS A PRIEST OR PRIESTESS REQUIRED AT TIME OF DEATH? No.

ANY OTHER PRACTICES OR TEACHINGS WHICH MAY CONFLICT WITH MILITARY DIRECTIVES

   OR PRACTICES: None, generally, though individual covens may have some.

   The local coven should be contacted if specific questions arise.

VII-8

AMERICAN COUNCIL OF WITCHES   Page 4

Basic Beliefs

BASIC TEACHINGS OR BELIEFS: Underlying agreements are summed up in the "Prin-
    ciples of Wiccan Beliefs" adopted by the American Council of Witches:
    (1) We practice Rites to attune ourselves with the natural rhythm of
    life forces marked by the Phases of the Moon and the Seasonal Quarters
    and Cross Quarters. (2) We recognize that our intelligence gives us a
    unique responsibility toward our environment. We seek to live in harmony
    with Nature, in ecological balance offering fulfillment to life and con-
    sciousness with an evolutionary concept. (3) We acknowledge a depth of
    power far greater than is apparent to the average person. Because it is
    far greater than ordinary, it is sometimes called "supernatural," but we
    see it as lying within that which is naturally potential to all. (4) We
    conceive the Creative Power in the Universe as manifesting through
    polarity - as masculine and feminine - and that this same Creative Power
    lives in all people, and functions through the interaction of the mascu-
    line and feminine. We value neither above the other, knowing each to be
    supportive of the other. We value Sex as pleasure, as the symbol and em-
    bodiment of life, and as one of the sources of energies used in magical
    practice and religious worship. (5) We recognize both outer worlds and
    inner or psychological worlds - sometimes known as the Spiritual World,
    the collective Unconscious, the Inner Planes, etc. - and we see the
    interaction of these two dimensions as the basis for paranormal phenomena
    and magical exercises. We neglect neither dimension for the other, see-
    ing both as necessary for our fulfillment. (6) We do not recognize any

BASIC BELIEFS (continued); authoritarian hierarchy, but do honor those who
   teach. respect those who share their greater knowledge and wisdom, and
   acknowledge those who have courageously given of themselves in leadership. (7) We see religion, magick, and wisdom-in-living as being united
   in the way one views the world and lives within it - a world-view and
   philosophy-of-life, which we identify as Witchcraft, the Wiccan way. (8)
   Calling oneself a "Witch" does not make a witch - but neither does he-
   redity itself, or the collecting of titles, degrees, and initiations. A
   Witch seeks to control the forces within him/herself that make life possible in order to live wisely and well without harm to others, and in
   harmony with Nature. (9) We acknowledge that it is the affirmation and
   fulfillment of life, in a continuation of evolution and development of
   consciousness, that gives meaning to the Universe we know, and to our
   personal role in it. (10) Our only animosity toward Christianity, or
   toward any other religion or philosophy-of-life, is to the extent that
   its institutions have claimed to be "the only way" and have sought to
   deny freedom to others and to suppress other ways of religious practice
   and belief. (11) As American Witches, we are not threatened by debates
   on the history of the Craft, the origins of various terms, the legiti-
   macy of various aspects of different traditions. We are concerned with
   the present, and our future. (12) We do not accept the concept of "absolute evil," nor do we worship any entity known as "Satan" or "the devil"
   as defined by the Christian tradition. We do not seek power through the

AMERICAN COUNCIL OF WITCHES   Page 6

Basic Beliefs, Literature, Ethics, Recruiting, Relationships

BASIC BELIEFS (continued): suffering of others, nor do we accept the concept

　　　that personal benefit can be only derived by denial to another. (13) We

　　　acknowledge that we seek within Nature for that which is contributory

　　　to our health and well-being.

　　　　　Specific expression of beliefs will vary widely, due to ethnic

　　　roots or the traditions of the individual coven.

CREEDAL STATEMENTS AND/OR AUTHORITATIVE LITERATURE: (See also "Basic Be-

　　　liefs") All witches use two books, a "grimore" or book of spells and

　　　magical procedures, and a "book of shadows" or book of ritual. Each

　　　coven will use a different grimore and/or book of shadows. One popular

　　　set are those published by Lady Sheba: The Grimore of Lady Sheba (St.

　　　Paul: Llewellyn Publications, 1972) and The Book of Shadows (St. Paul:

　　　Llewellyn Publications, 1973).

ETHICAL PRACTICES: Wiccan ethics are summed up in the law called the Wiccan

　　　Rede, "An Ye Harm None, Do As Ye Will."

HOW DOES WITCHCRAFT RECRUIT NEW MEMBERS? Witches do not *proselytize*, but

　　　welcome inquiries from those who hear about the Craft by either word of

　　　mouth or the media.

RELATIONSHIP WITH OTHER RELIGIONS: Cooperation with the whole *Pagan* community

　　　is very high. Relations with other religions are cordial, except those

　　　groups which have sought to persecute and defame the Craft.

BAHA'I FAITH
Baha'i National Center
112 Linden Avenue
Wilmette, Illinois 60091

National Spiritual Assembly of the
Baha'is of the United States
Mr. Glenford E. Mitchell, Secretary

HISTORICAL ROOTS: In Persia, in 1844, Mirza 'Ali Muhammad (known as the Bab
which means the "Gate"), the Prophet-Herald of the Baha'i Faith, announced that His mission was to prepare mankind for the coming of a new, world
Prophet. Nineteen years later, in 1863, Mirza Husayn 'Ali (known as
Baha'u'llah which means the "Glory of God") announced that He was the
Prophet of Whom the Bab had spoken. Baha'u'llah spent forty years in
prison and exile for his religious teachings. He died in 1892 still a
religious prisoner. His son, 'Abdu'l-Baha, Who had also been imprisoned
with His Father since the age of nine, was named in Baha'u'llah's Will
and Testament as His Successor. In 1921, 'Abdu'l-Baha died and in His
Will appointed His grandson, Shoghi Effendi, as the Guardian of the
Baha'i Faith and thus its leader.

CURRENT WOLRD LEADERS: Before his death in 1957, Shoghi Effendi had aided the
Baha'i Faith to expand sufficiently so that its institutions were capable
of administering its affairs. Today the Baha'i world community is governed by a body of nine men elected every five years by the Baha'i National Assemblies. This body is called the Universal House of Justice
and is located in Haifa, Israel. It rules on those things not expressly
covered in the Writings of Baha'u'llah and is considered infallible in
these matters.

ORIGINS IN THE U.S.: The first formal mention of the Baha'i Faith was at the
Columbian Exposition held in Chicago in 1893. The first Baha'i group was
formed in Chicago the following year and shortly afterward numerous communities appeared throughout the country. Notable expansion occurred in

BAHA'I FAITH	Page 2
Origins, Organization, Leadership, Worship	

ORIGINS (continued): 1912 when 'Abdu'l-Baha, Who had been released from jail

in 1908, spent several months traveling coast-to-coast proclaiming the

Baha'i Faith. Today the National Spiritual Assembly of the Baha'is of

the United States meets in Wilmette, Illinois, where the Baha'i National

Center for the U.S. is located.

NUMBER OF ADHERENTS IN THE U.S.: It is a policy not to give the exact member-

ship figures, but Baha'is reside in over 5,900 localities in the U.S.

(over 70,000 in the world), and there are over 980 local spiritual as-

semblies (communities with nine or more adult Baha'is) in the U.S. (over

17,000 in the world).

ORGANIZATIONAL STRUCTURE: The Baha'i Administrative Order, whose structure is

delineated in the sacred texts, safeguards the Faith against division.

The framework of the Administrative Order consists of institutions elec-

ted by a process which excludes parties or factions, and all electioneer-

ing practices. The basic institution is the local spiritual assembly

which is elected directly in every locality where nine or more Baha'is

over 21 reside. Then there are national spiritual assemblies elected by

means of delegates. Both the local and national assemblies are elected

once a year and consist of nine members. The international governing

body is the Universal House of Justice (see also "Current World Leaders").

LEADERSHIP AND ROLE OF PRIESTHOOD: There are no clergy in the Baha'i Faith

(see also "Organizational Structure".)

WHO MAY CONDUCT WORSHIP SERVICES? The individual Baha'is, children as well

as adults, plan and conduct their worship services.

BAHA'I FAITH   Page 3

Worship, Requirements

IS WORSHIP REQUIRED? No, but Baha'is are encouraged to pray as a group as

   well as individually since this strengthens them as a group and lends

   force to their prayer.

WORSHIP REQUIREMENTS: The first day of each of the nineteen months of nine-

   teen days that make up the Baha'i calendar is the regular time for a

   Baha'i community to gather for the purpose of worship, conducting com-

   munity business, and socializing; this gathering is called a nineteen-

   day "Feast."

MINIMUM EQUIPMENT FOR WORSHIP: None, although Baha'is will use Baha'i prayer

   books and other Baha'i books containing sacred texts for their prayers

   and meditations.

FACILITIES FOR WORSHIP: Baha'is have no churches. The Baha'i Houses of Wor-

   ship are not churches; they symbolize the basic idea of unity that under-

   lies the Baha'i Faith. It is not necessary to be in any special place

   for worship.

OTHER SPECIFIC RELIGIOUS REQUIREMENTS OTHER THAN WORSHIP: Baha'is are re-

   quired to live a life in accordance with Baha'u'llah's teachings and

   laws, to pray and meditate daily, to give to the Baha'i Fund, and to

   teach others about Baha'u'llah's message to mankind. They are also com-

   manded to work, and work performed in the spirit of service to mankind

   is regarded as worship.

DIETARY LAWS OR RESTRICTIONS: None. However, Baha'is are prohibited from

   using alcoholic beverages, narcotics, or other habit-forming drugs ex-

   cept when given for medical reasons.

VII-14

BAHA'I FAITH	Page 4
Holidays, Position on Service	

SPECIAL RELIGIOUS HOLIDAYS: Besides the Baha'i "Feast," Baha'is observe a
nineteen-day fast beginning March 2 and ending March 21. Holy Days are:
Festival of Ridvan, April 21-May 2, celebrating the period during which
Baha'u'llah announced that He was the Promised One; Declaration of the
Bab, May 23; Ascension of Baha'u'llah, May 29; Martyrdom of the Bab,
July 9; Birth of the Bab, October 20; Birth of Baha'u'llah, November 12;
the Ascension of 'Abdu'l-Baha, November 28; and Naw-Ruz (New Year),
March 21. If possible, Baha'is should suspend work on all of the Holy
Days except November 28.

FUNERAL AND BURIAL REQUIREMENTS: If possible, a Baha'i or Baha'i community
should take part in the funeral arrangements or at least for the necessary funeral prayers. The body is not to be embalmed unless state law
requires. Interment must take place within an hour's travel time from
the place of death.

AUTOPSY: Generally permitted.

CREMATION: Forbidden.

MEDICAL TREATMENT: No restrictions.

UNIFORM APPEARANCE REQUIREMENTS: No required distinctive clothing or insig-
nia. Many Baha'is will wear a ring with a specific Baha'i symbol on it,
but it is not required. Baha'is are enjoined to be clean and to dress
with propriety, modesty, and taste.

POSITION ON SERVICE IN THE ARMED FORCES: Baha'i teachings require that
Baha'is obey the laws of the government under which they live. This
requirement includes the obligation of military service. However,

BAHA'I FAITH	Page 5

Position on Service, Basic Beliefs, Literature

POSITION ON SERVICE (continued): Baha'is are also required to apply for
noncombatant service whenever the opportunity to do so is legally provided by their government on the basis of religious training and belief.

IS A PRIEST REQUIRED AT THE TIME OF DEATH? No.

ANY OTHER PRACTICES OR TEACHINGS WHICH MAY CONFLICT WITH MILITARY DIRECTIVES
OR PRACTICE: None.

BASIC TEACHINGS OR BELIEFS: The Baha'i Faith is centered on three principles:
the oneness of God, the oneness of religion, and the oneness of mankind.
This Faith is summarized in the teachings of Baha'u'llah who emphasized:
the independent investigation of truth; the essential harmony of science
and religion; the equality of men and women; the elimination of preju-
dices of all kinds; universal compulsory education; a spiritual solution
to the economic problems of the world; a universal auxiliary language;
and universal peace upheld by a world government.

   Baha'is believe that each Prophet or Manifestation of God is the
focal point of spiritual light and life for mankind in the age in which
He comes. In this age, the focal center of spiritual guidance for mankind is Baha'u'llah. His Revelation will aid mankind to attain "the
Kingdom of God on earth."

CREEDAL STATEMENTS AND/OR AUTHORITATIVE LITERATURE: All the Writings of the
Bab, Baha'u'llah, and 'Abdu'l-Baha are regarded as Baha'i sacred texts.
In addition, all the works of the Guardian, Shoghi Effendi, and the
Universal House of Justice are regarded as infallible guidance and
interpretation.

BAHA'I FAITH	Page 6

Ethics, Recruiting, Relationships

ETHICAL PRACTICES: Baha'is are expected to live lives of high moral conduct

and rectitude, and to be living examples of the Baha'i spirit.

Baha'u'llah has given much guidance, both generally and specifically, in

His Writings as to what the Baha'i life should be like. The Universal

House of Justice continues to give guidance on issues not specifically

mentioned in Baha'u'llah's Writings.

HOW DOES THE BAHA'I FAITH RECRUIT MEMBERS? Each Baha'i is responsible for

giving the message of Baha'u'llah to the best of his/her ability; this

includes living a Baha'i life as well as spreading the Faith by word of

mouth, through literature, the media, etc. Baha'is are forbidden to

proselytize.

RELATIONSHIP WITH OTHER RELIGIONS: Baha'is are directed to associate with

the followers of other religions with fellowship, unity, and accord.

The individual Baha'i, the local, and the national Baha'i communities are

allowed to join with other religions in organizations whose aims and pur-

poses are in accord with Baha'i principles, especially that of unity.

NOTE: In actual usage, the Baha'i Faith uses acute accents throughout their

writing to indicate appropriate word usage. These include, for ex-

ample, Bahá'í, Mírzá 'Alí, Báb, Bahá'u'lláh, and 'Abdu'l-Bahá.

CHURCH OF SATAN
Post Office Box 7633
San Francisco, California 94120

Anton S. LaVey
High Priest

AKA: Satanists

HISTORICAL ROOTS: The Church of Satan is an *eclectic* body that traces

its origin to many sources - classical voodoo, the Hell-Fire Club

of eighteenth century England, the ritual magic of Aleister Crowley,

and the Black Order of Germany in the 1920s and 1930s. It departs

from its predecessors by (1) its organization into a church, and

(2) the openness of its magical endeavors.

CURRENT WORLD LEADER: Anton Szandor LaVey, High Priest.

ORIGINS IN THE U.S.: The Church of Satan was formed on Walpurgisnacht,

April 30, 1966, in San Francisco, California, when Anton LaVey pro-

claimed the beginning of the Satanic Era. Initial growth came from

coverage in the mass media. Articles included coverage of LaVey hold-

ing a funeral for a member of the U.S. Navy killed in San Francisco.

NUMBER OF ADHERENTS IN THE U.S.: Between 10,000 and 20,000.

ORGANIZATIONAL STRUCTURE: The Church of Satan is focused in the Central

Grotto in San Francisco. It accepts or rejects all potential members

and charters other grottos (congregations) around the country. Iso-

lated individuals relate directly to the Central Grotto. Power to

regulate members is in the hands of the Head of the Church.

LEADERSHIP AND ROLE OF PRIESTS: The Priesthood of the Church of Satan is

not comprised of individuals who are necessarily adept in the perfor-

mance of rituals, though pastoral and organizational abilities are not

minimized. The rank of Priest is conferred on those who have achieved

CHURCH OF SATAN	Page 2

Leadership, Worship

LEADERSHIP AND ROLE OF PRIESTS (continued): a measurable degree of esteem or
   proficiency and/or success; one's level of membership within the Church
   is commensurate with his/her position outside the Church. Hence, a
   respected career soldier or Commissioned Officer in the Army might
   qualify, though be totally uninvolved with group activity. This form
   of stratification determines the leadership and selects the governing
   body of the Church. Rituals are conducted by a de facto priest, i.e.,
   a celebrant member who has evidenced a working knowledge of and ability
   to conduct services and is authorized by the Central Grotto.

WHO MAY CONDUCT A RITUAL? Anyone, but a priest is required for group
   worship.

IS GROUP WORSHIP REQUIRED? No, but it is strongly encouraged, because it is
   a strong reinforcement of the faith and instillation of power.

WORSHIP REQUIREMENTS: Worship in the Church of Satan is based upon the belief that man needs ritual, dogma, fantasy, and enchantment. Worship
   consists of magical rituals and there are three basic kinds: sexual
   rituals, to fulfill a desire; compassionate rituals, to help another;
   and destructive rituals, used for anger, annoyance or hate. Grottos
   often gather on Friday evenings for group rituals.

MINIMUM EQUIPMENT FOR WORSHIP: Varies with the type of ritual performed
   but is likely to include a black robe, an altar, the symbol of Baphomet
   (Satan), candles, a bell, a *chalice*, elixer (wine or some other drink
   most pleasing to the palate), a sword, a model phallus, a gong, and
   parchment.

CHURCH OF SATAN	Page 3

Worship, Holidays, Requirements

FACILITIES FOR WORSHIP: A private place where an altar can be erected and rituals performed.

OTHER SPECIFIC RELIGIOUS REQUIREMENTS OTHER THAN WORSHIP: None.

DIETARY LAWS OR RESTRICTIONS: None.

SPECIAL RELIGIOUS HOLIDAYS: The Highest holiday in the Satanic religion is one's own birthday. Every man is a God as he chooses to recognize that fact. After one's birthday, Walpurgisnacht (April 30) and Halloween are most important. April 30 is the grand climax of the spring equinox and Halloween was one of the times of the great fire festivals among the ancient Druids. The *solstices* and *equinoxes*--which fall in March, June, September, and December and mark the first day of the new seasons--are also celebrated.

FUNERAL AND BURIAL REQUIREMENTS: The priests of the Church of Satan perform funerals, and the Central Grotto should be contacted in case of death.

AUTOPSY: No restrictions.

CREMATIONS: Only permitted in extreme circumstances, such as an expedient measure where it is necessary to safeguard the health of others.

MEDICAL TREATMENT: No restrictions.

UNIFORM APPEARANCE REQUIREMENTS: No restrictions.

POSITION ON SERVICE IN THE ARMED FORCES: None.

IS A PRIEST REQUIRED AT TIME OF DEATH? No.

ANY OTHER PRACTICES OR TEACHINGS WHICH MAY CONFLICT WITH MILITARY DIRECTIVES OR PRACTICES: None.

CHURCH OF SATAN   Page 4

Basic Beliefs, Literature, Ethics

BASIC TEACHINGS OR BELIEFS: The Church of Satan worships Satan, most clearly

symbolized in the Roman God Lucifer, the bearer of light, the spirit of

the air, and the personification of enlightenment. Satan is not visua-

lized as an *anthropomorphic* being, rather he represents the forces of

nature. To the Satanist, the self is the highest embodiment of human

life and is sacred. The Church of Satan is essentially a human poten-

tial movement, and members are encouraged to develop whatever capabilities

they can by which they might excel. They are, however, cautioned to

recognized their limitations -- an important factor in this philosophy

of rational self-interest. Satanists practice magick, the art of

changing situations or events in accordance with one's will, which

would, using normally accepted methods, be impossible.

CREEDAL STATEMENTS AND/OR AUTHORITATIVE LITERATURE: The writings of Anton S.

LeVey provide the direction for the Satanists -- The Satanic Bible,

The Compleat Witch, and The Satanic Rituals. (See also "Ethical

Practices.") Members are encouraged to study pertinent writings which

serve as guidelines for Satanic thought, such as works of Mark Twain,

Niccolo Machiavelli, G.S. Shaw, Ayn Rand, Friedrich Nietzsche, etc.

ETHICAL PRACTICES: The ethical stance of the Church of Satan is summarized

in the Nine Satanic Statements: "(1) Satan represents indulgence, in-

stead of abstinence!; (2) Satan represents vital existence, instead of

spiritual pipe dreams!; (3) Satan represents undefiled wisdom, instead

of hypocritical self-deceit!; (4) Satan represents kindness to those

CHURCH OF SATAN   Page 5

Ethics, Recruiting, Relationships

ETHICAL PRACTICES (continued): who deserve it, instead of love wasted on

ingrates!; (5) Satan represents vengeance, instead of turning the other

cheek!; (6) Satan represents responsibility for the responsible, in-

stead of concern for psychic vampires!; (7) Satan represents man as

just another animal, sometimes better, more often worse than those that

walk on all fours, who, because of his 'divine and intellectual devel-

opment' has become the most vicious animal of all!; (8) Satan repre-

sents all of the so-called sins, as they lead to physical, mental, or

emotional gratification!; (9) Satan has been the best friend the church

has ever had, as he has kept it in business all these years!"

Beyond the above principles, Satanists generally oppose the use

of narcotics which dull the senses, and suicide, which cuts off life

(the great indulgence), and stand firmly for law and order. The Church

of Satan is not to be confused with "Satanist" groups which have been

found to engage in illegal acts.

HOW DOES THE CHURCH OF SATAN RECRUIT NEW MEMBERS? The Church does not

proselytize but welcomes inquiries from honest potential Satanists

who hear about the Church from the various books about it, the mass

media or word-of-mouth. New members must go through a screening

process before they are accepted.

RELATIONSHIP WITH OTHER RELIGIONS: The Church of Satan stands as a gather-

ing point for all those who believe in what the Christian Church opposes,

CHURCH OF SATAN   Page 6

Relationships

RELATIONSHIP WITH OTHER RELIGIONS (continued): and members are generally

   hostile to its teachings and resultant behavior patterns. To a lesser

   extent, the same position holds for Eastern religions.

CHURCHES OF SCIENTOLOGY
New American Saint Hill Organization
2005 West Ninth
Los Angeles, California 90813

Mr. Greg Taylor
Ministry of Information
Church of Scientology
2125 S Street, N.W.
Washington, D.C. 20008

HISTORICAL ROOTS: L. Ron Hubbard, philosopher and writer, resigned his com-
mission as a U.S. Naval Officer in the 1940's to devote his time to
producing a study of the human mind. His efforts resulted in a book,
Dianetics: The Modern Science of Mental Health. Further study into the
spiritual nature of man, including a primary emphasis on Eastern religious perspectives, led to the discoveries which were collectively
named Scientology.

CURRENT WORLD LEADER: The Rev. Jane Kember, Guardian.

ORIGINS IN THE U.S.: Hubbard founded the Hubbard Association of Scientologists International (HASI) in Arizona in 1952. HASI's efforts led to
the overseas expansion of Scientology to England, current location of
the Scientology international headquarters. Further organizational development led to the incorporation of the Founding Church of Scientology
in Washington, D.C., in 1955. Later expansion saw the U.S. headquarters
move to the present California location as the Church of Scientology of
California.

NUMBER OF ADHERENTS IN THE U.S.: Approximately 3 million.

ORGANIZATIONAL STRUCTURE: The international leadership of the Church (in
England) is located in the International Board of Scientology Organization, the Board of Directors of the Churches of Scientology and the
Guardian. The International Board is concerned with the worldwide
propagation of the faith and its viability, issues doctrinal directives
and advice of a technical nature. It sets ministerial standards and

CHURCHES OF SCIENTOLOGY	Page 2
Organization, Leadership, Holidays	

ORGANIZATIONAL STRUCTURE (continued): administrative policy. The Guardian

and Board of Directors appoint local directors of Scientology Churches.

At present there are 24 churches, 3 senior organizations, and 98 mis-

sions included in the Church of Scientology in the U.S.

In the United States, the Church of Scientology of California func-

tions as headquarters and senior eccesiastical body. Each local Church

of Scientology is headed by an independent Board of Directors and by an

Assistant Guardian appointed by the Guardian. Though autonomous in

organization, each Church shares a common doctrine, practice, and belief.

LEADERSHIP AND ROLE OF MINISTERS: Ministers perform wedding ceremonies,

naming ceremonies, and funerals. Ministers also conduct Sunday Church

Services and deliver pastoral counselling to the Church's parishioners.

WHO MAY CONDUCT SERVICES? Ordained ministers.

IS GROUP WORSHIP REQUIRED? No.

WORSHIP REQUIREMENTS: None, but regular weekly services are offered at the

local Churches of Scientology.

MINIMUM EQUIPMENT FOR WORSHIP: None.

FACILITIES FOR WORSHIP: None.

OTHER SPECIFIC REQUIREMENTS FOR WORSHIP: None.

DIETARY LAWS OR RESTRICTIONS: None.

SPECIAL RELIGIOUS HOLIDAYS: Two holidays are celebrated annually by the

Church of Scientology: International Scientology Day (Sept. 1) and

International Auditors Day (Sept. 14). At irregular intervals, Prayer

CHURCHES OF SCIENTOLOGY	Page 3

Requirements, Creedal Statements

SPECIAL RELIGIOUS HOLIDAYS (continued): Day is held as a time to reaffirm

    faith in the principles of Scientology and celebrate growth and progress.

FUNERAL AND BURIAL REQUIREMENTS: The Church of Scientology holds funeral

    services for its members and publishes a funeral service among its

    ceremonies. There are no special burial or funeral facilities re-

    quired, however.

AUTOPSY: No restrictions.

CREMATION: No restrictions.

MEDICAL TREATMENT: Generally no restrictions. The Creed of Scientology, how-

    ever, generally opposes the treatment of mental illness in a non-

    religious context.

UNIFORM APPEARANCE REQUIREMENTS: None.

POSITION ON SERVICE IN THE ARMED FORCES: None.

IS A PRIEST OR CLERGY PERSON REQUIRED AT THE TIME OF DEATH? No, but desired.

ANY OTHER PRACTICES OR TEACHINGS WHICH MAY CONFLICT WITH MILITARY DIRECTIVES

    OR PRACTICES: None.

CREEDAL STATEMENTS AND/OR AUTHORITATIVE LITERATURE: The Creed of the Church

    states: "We of the Church believe: That all men of whatever race,

    colour or creed were created with equal rights. That all men have

    inalienable rights to their own religious practices and their performance.

    That all men have inalienable rights to their own lives. That all men

    have inalienable rights to their sanity. That all men have inalienable

    rights to their own defense. That all men have inalienable rights to

CHURCHES OF SCIENTOLOGY   Page 4

Creedal Statements, Literature

CREEDAL STATEMENTS AND/OR AUTHORITATIVE LITERATURE (continued): conceive,

choose, assist, and support their own organizations, churches, and gov-

ernments. That all men have inalienable rights to think freely, to talk

freely, to write freely their own opinions and to counter utter or write

upon the opinions of others. That all men have inalienable rights to

the creation of their own kinds. That the souls of men have the rights

of men. That the study of the mind and the healing of mentally-caused

ills should not be alienated from religion or condoned in non-religious

fields. And that no agency less than God has the power to suspend or

set aside these rights, overtly or covertly.

"And we of the Church believe: That man is basically good. That

he is seeking to survive. That his survival depends upon himself and

upon his fellows, and his attainment of brotherhood with the Universe.

"And we of the Church believe that the laws of God forbid Man: To

destroy his own kind. To destroy the sanity of another. To destroy or

enslave another's soul. To destroy or reduce the survival of one's

companions or one's group.

"And we of the Church believe: That the Spirit can be saved and

That the Spirit alone may save or heal the body."

The Church has published several texts: The Background and Cere-

monies of the Church of Scientology of California, Worldwide (The Church

of Scientology World Wide, 1970), Scientology: A World Religion Emerges

in the Space Age (Church of Scientology Information Service/Department of

CHURCHES OF SCIENTOLOGY	Page 5
Literature, Basic Beliefs	

CREEDAL STATEMENTS AND/OR AUTHORITATIVE LITERATURE (continued): Archives,
   1974), and <u>Evidence on Religious Bona Fides and Status of the Church
   of Scientology</u> (Department of Archives, U.S. Ministry of Public Relations, n.d.). All new members of the Church are urged to read <u>Dianetics:
   The Modern Science of Mental Health</u> by L. Ron Hubbard (available in
   several editions).

BASIC TEACHINGS OR BELIEFS: Scientology is a religious philosophy which has
   roots in Eastern religious perspectives, which start with the concept
   of Man as a spiritual agent and deal with man's encumbrances, his aspi-
   rations, and the practical means through which he then attains individual salvation. From self-realization and spiritual awareness comes
   harmonious integration with other Life Forms, the Physical Universe and
   the Supreme Being.

      Basic to the teachings of Scientology are the concepts of soul and
   mind. Each person in Scientology discovers himself to be a Thetan, a
   soul, an individual force. The Thetan is the person himself immortal,
   and fully responsible. The Thetan controls the Body. Scientology
   teaches that people are basically good and seeking to survive, but are
   hindered from doing so by painful past experiences and harmful acts
   against other. To the degree that one attains self-knowledge, they will
   increase ability to survive. The mind is the storehouse of mental pictures and all the Thetan has ever seen, felt, heard or done, and is
   used by the Thetan for evaluation and computation. Mental image pictures

CHURCHES OF SCIENTOLOGY   Page 6

Basic Beliefs, Ethical Practices, Recruiting, Relationships

BASIC TEACHINGS OR BELIEFS (continued): containing elements of pain and un-
consciousness ("engrams") are stored in that part of the mind called the
Reactive Mind. The engrams, when reactivated, can reimpose their ten-
sions in the present. By pastoral counseling ("auditing"), engrams can
be removed, and a state of self-determination ("clear") be acquired.

ETHICAL PRACTICES: Found in two ethical codes, the "Code of a Scientologist,"
and the "Code of Honor." Both are based upon the principle of "Reason
and contemplation of optimum survival." Any ethical decision considered
"right action" would at the same time enhance survival for the maximum
area of life (i.e., the individual, family, group, mankind, other life
forms, spiritual awareness, and the Supreme Being). This doctrine is an
expansion of the principle of "the greatest good for the greatest number"
to include all sectors of existence.

HOW DOES THE CHURCH OF SCIENTOLOGY RECRUIT MEMBERS? The Church of Scientology
has an aggressive program of recruitment that includes the distribution
of literature, leafleting, invitations to public events and word-of-mouth
reports by Scientologists to their acquaintances.

LATIONSHIP WITH OTHER RELIGIONS: The Church of Scientology is non-denomina-
tional, i.e., is open to people of all religious beliefs.

THE FOUNDATION FAITH OF THE MILLENIUM
1147 First Avenue   Father Raphael
New York, New York   10021

(name changed to The Foundation Faith of God as of December, 1977)

HISTORICAL ROOTS: In 1963, a group of professionals of several nationalities
   from the U.S., Canada, and Europe came together to initiate a movement
   which was to become the Foundation Faith of the Millenium. From 1963 to
   1974, they worked extensively in the social service field, including individual and group counseling and the establishment of centers in a number
   of American cities (providing a community coffeehouse, courses and lectures, and services).

   The group's formative religious experience took place in 1966. In a
   type of religious retreat, the group (30 members) lived in a place called
   Xtul on the Yucatan peninsula. This period of intense examination was a
   time of religious and spiritual revelation for both the total group and
   for its individual members. A time of great ascetism, it functioned much
   as the Exodus did for the Jews. From this period came the strong and
   simple belief which forms the basis of the Foundation Faith.

CURRENT WORLD LEADERS: There is no single "leader" as such. From the Council
   of Luminaries (See "Organizational Structure"), four senior members are
   elected annually as an executive committee to oversee the administration
   and organization of the Foundation Faith.

ORIGINS IN THE U.S.: (See also "Historical Roots.") The group first started
   working in New Orleans in 1967. The Foundation Faith of the Millenium
   was incorporated in New York State in 1974.

NUMBER OF ADHERENTS IN THE U.S.: Approximately 20,000 with a direct religious
   affiliation, and more than 500,000 affiliated with the many programs,
   primarily educational, sponsored and organized by the Foundation Faith.

THE FOUNDATION FAITH OF THE MILLENIUM   Page 2

Organization, Leadership, Worship

ORGANIZATIONAL STRUCTURE: The Foundation Faith is organized along strict

hierarchical lines, with ministers gaining seniority according to their

experience and ability. The ranks of the ministry are: (1) Ordained

Ministers, known as Father or Mother, including Luminaries, Minor Lumi-

naries, and Celebrants; (2) Regular Ministers, known as Brother or Sister,

including Mentors and Covenanters; and (3) Ministers-in-Training, includ-

ing Witnesses and Aspirants. The Council of Luminaries (currently 15

members) is the governing body, and consists of all Luminaries and Minor

Luminaries. A minister promoted to Minor Luminary automatically becomes

a member of the Council.

Ranks also exist within the laity, the most common being Lay Founder.

These may serve as lay minister after instruction by a minister.

The Foundation Faith is administered internationally from its New

York headquarters. Other branches consist of both ministerial teams and

lay members who conduct activities in the absence of ministerial personnel.

LEADERSHIP AND ROLE OF MINISTERS: (See also "Organizational Structure.") All

ministers may conduct all services held by the Foundation Faith. Women

occupy and have the same opportunity to occupy all positions open to men.

As the Foundation Faith expands, greater responsibility likely will be

delegated to the laity for conducting local affairs in a number of cities.

WHO MAY CONDUCT SERVICES? All ministers, and certain lay members after due

instruction from a full-time minister.

IS GROUP WORSHIP REQUIRED? No. Group worship occurs daily at all branches.

In cities or areas where no center exists, individual worship on a

personal basis is encouraged.

THE FOUNDATION FAITH OF THE MILLENIUM	Page 3
Worship, Requirements, Holidays	

WORSHIP REQUIREMENTS: The main religious service is on Saturday evening, as Saturday is the Sabbath for The Foundation Faith. Other services occur daily, and members also hold morning and evening prayer, usually in the form of private prayer.

MINIMUM EQUIPMENT FOR WORSHIP: None for individual worshipers. A group meeting in communal worship requires: a table to serve as an altar, bowls to contain fire and water, candles in a specific arrangement, incense, a Foundation symbol (logo of the Faith), and chairs for the congregation.

FACILITIES FOR WORSHIP: For an individual, a private, quiet room. For groups, a room is required where equipment can be set up on a permanent basis, and which members can visit for private prayer and meditation.

OTHER SPECIFIC RELIGIOUS REQUIREMENTS OTHER THAN WORSHIP: No specific requirements. However, The Foundation Faith is active in the field of personal development and communication. It conducts numerous workshops in this area to help individuals.

DIETARY LAWS OR RESTRICTIONS: No specific restrictions. Members are encouraged to eat a healthy and balanced diet, utilizing health foods and vitamin supplements wherever possible.

SPECIAL RELIGIOUS HOLIDAYS: May 20th (Foundation Day) and November 20th (Founder's Day). Founders take the day off work, and, if near a center, take part in religious services and festivals. Covenant Month (October 20 - November 20), while not a holiday per se, commemorates the original religious experience of the group. Considerable activity takes place in all branches at that time.

THE FOUNDATION FAITH OF THE MILLENIUM   Page 4

Requirements, Position on Service

FUNERAL AND BURIAL REQUIREMENTS: There is a specified funeral service, to be
    conducted by a Foundation Faith minister. When this is impossible, the
    Faith recognizes the validity of services conducted by most denominations
    for this purpose. If an individual member requests it, his body is
    brought to a Foundation Faith center for the service, or a memorial
    service is held after a burial in a foreign land.

AUTOPSY: No restrictions.

CREMATION: Individual choice; no restrictions.

MEDICAL TREATMENT: Generally no restrictions. However, one of the principle
    activities of The Foundation Faith is in its healing ministry, both mental
    and physical healing. The former takes place through counseling, the
    latter through the laying on of hands. The Foundation Faith conducts a
    number of services devoted specifically to healing.

UNIFORM APPEARANCE REQUIREMENTS: None.

POSITION ON SERVICE IN THE ARMED FORCES: Service in defense of family and
    homeland is accepted as a necessity, but wars not directly fulfilling this
    function (Vietnam is cited as an example) are not condoned. The Faith
    fully supports ministers and members objecting to service in a theater
    such as Vietnam. War is viewed as a necessity arising out of man's
    alienation from God. Killing, including killing animals, is abhorred.
    The Foundation Faith recognizes the sanctity of all life as created by
    God and not to be taken by man.

IS A MINISTER REQUIRED AT THE TIME OF DEATH? No, but preferred if possible.

THE FOUNDATION FAITH OF THE MILLENIUM   Page 5
Basic Beliefs, Literature

ANY OTHER PRACTICES OR TEACHINGS WHICH MAY CONFLICT WITH MILITARY DIRECTIVES

   OR PRACTICE: None (see also "Position on Service in the Armed Forces").

BASIC TEACHINGS OR BELIEFS: The Foundation Faith believes that the world and

   mankind were created by God, named as Jehovah in certain versions of the

   Bible. God loves His people, and is manifest in history in the reward and

   punishment of His people. The world is beset with problems, both personal

   and social, and the only true answer is life devoted to God. It believes

   that God sent many prophets into the world to different races and

   cultures, to lead men to God, and to teach them to live according to God's

   laws, exemplified by the 10 Commandments.

       Much of the teaching is derived from the Bible, specifically the Old

   Testament, but the validity of all religions which direct men to lead a

   good life devoted to the service of God and adherence to His laws is

   recognized. God and His teachings are seen as manifest in many different

   religions. Christ, Moses, Mohammed, Buddha, etc., were all sent by God

   to lead men to Him. Many major religions foresee the coming of a

   messianic figure (known by many different names) to lead mankind into a

   new age or millenium (hence, the Faith's name) ruled over by God and His

   laws. The Foundation Faith believes that these are the End Times, and

   within these times the Messiah, a representative of God, will appear in

   human form to lead men back to God.

CREEDAL STATEMENTS AND/OR AUTHORITATIVE LITERATURE: Creedal statements appear

   in the specific ritual of the Foundation Faith. The Bible is regarded as

   a major source of authority, and commentaries and/or articles regarding

THE FOUNDATION FAITH OF THE MILLENIUM   Page 6

Ethics, Recruiting, Relationships

CREEDAL STATEMENTS AND/OR AUTHORITATIVE LITERATURE (continued): the beliefs

of the Foundation Faith appear in pamphlet form and in the periodicals

published by the Faith.

ETHICAL PRACTICES: Normal stipulations as required for a "good life," follow-

ing basic guidelines set down in the Bible and other holy literature.

HOW DOES THE FOUNDATION FAITH RECRUIT MEMBERS? The Foundation Faith does not

proselytize, but it does propagate its views and beliefs through its

literature and a nationally syndicated radio program. It seeks to provide

spiritual and moral leadership, and to encourage a lifestyle devoted to

God and the following of His laws. The Foundation Faith provides facil-

ities and activities designed to fulfill and interest the individual and

to allow him/her to decide for themselves, based on that experience. No

conflict is seen when members belong to the Foundation Faith and yet

continue to take part in their denomination of upbringing.

RELATIONSHIP WITH OTHER RELIGIONS: (See also "How Does the Foundation Faith

Recruit Members?") The Foundation Faith has joined in a number of

cooperative ventures with other denominations, particularly in the

area of the media, including public broadcasting. Individual ministers

have served on a number of cooperative ministerial boards and commit-

tees in several American cities.

GARDNERIAN WICCA
c/o Lady Theos
P.O. Box 56
Commack, L.I., New York 11725

Lady Theos
High Priestess

HISTORICAL ROOTS: Witchcraft or Wicca is the Old Religion, the tribal worship
of ancient peoples based in magick, herbology, healing, and the worship
(primarily) of the Mother Goddess and (secondarily) her consort, the
Horned God. Witches have existed throughout known history in many parts
of the world. The term "witch," more properly "wicca," comes from the
Anglo Saxon word for "wise." Wicca's marked revival in the 20th Century
is largely due to such scholars as Margaret A. Murray, who traced the
existence of the Old Pagan Religion in pre-historic Europe. At the fore-
front of this revival is Gerald Gardner, the famous witch of the Isle of
Man.

After years in the east, Gardner returned to England in the 1930s,
located a Wicca group, and was initiated by "Old Dorothy" Clutterbuck. He
participated in the "Operation Cone of Power" during World War II, in
which English witches joined forces to turn back Hitler's invasion of
England. In 1949, he published High Magic's Aid, a novel about Medieval
Wicca based on his growing knowledge of 20th Century Witchcraft. After
repeal of the last anti-Witchcraft law in Britain in 1951, Gardner became
publically prominent. He opened a Museum of Witchcraft on the Isle of
Man, and in 1954 published Witchcraft Today in which he attacked the idea
that Wicca was the worship of Satan and declared himself a witch, devoted
to the Mother Goddess. As a result, many witches associated with him and
other people contacted him to join the Craft. Those who associated with
Gardner, who shared his views of Wicca, and who started to use the rituals
he used have come to be called "Gardnerians."

GARDNERIAN WICCA	Page 2
Leadership, Origin in U.S., Organization, Worship	

CURRENT WORLD LEADER: (See also "Historical Roots.") No formal leader. In the U.S., most Gardnerians recognize as national leaders High Priestess Lady Theos and her High Priest Phoenix.

ORIGINS IN THE U.S.: Brought to the U.S. by Lady Rowen and her High Priest Robat from England in 1962. Raised in the Church of England, they began to read books on the Craft and eventually to correspond with Gardner. They travelled to the Isle of Man a number of times and were fully initiated, then began to form a coven in the U.S. Lady Theos succeeded Lady Rowen upon her retirement in 1972.

NUMBER OF ADHERENTS IN THE U.S.: Figures are not generally published, but estimates range between 2,500 and 5,000.

ORGANIZATIONAL STRUCTURE: Each coven is autonomous, headed by a High Priestess and her High Priest. Covens vary in size from 8 to 14 members. The High Priestess heads the coven. The High Priestess who trained her is recognized as a Queen to whom she can turn for counsel and advise, thus maintaining a lineage of High Priestesses throughout Gardnerian Wicca. Members pass through three initiations, each of which must be at least a year and a day apart. Covens are organized in pairs of males and females.

LEADERSHIP AND ROLE OF PRIESTESS/PRIEST: The High Priestess and her High Priest are responsible for coven activities, serving both as leaders in the rituals and as teachers for coven members.

WHO MAY CONDUCT WORSHIP SERVICES? Only a High Priestess can cast a circle.

IS GROUP WORSHIP REQUIRED? Generally, yes. Individual worship is possible, but not generally practiced.

GARDNERIAN WICCA   Page 3

Worship, Holidays, Requirements

MINIMUM EQUIPMENT FOR WORSHIP: An atheme (ritual knife), a bowl of water, a

    censer with incense, salt, an altar and 6 candles in candlesticks. A

    sword and pentacle (talisman) are optional, not widely used. All tools

    must be ritually consecrated by a High Priestess.

FACILITIES FOR WORSHIP: Private location in which a circle nine feet in dia-

    meter can be drawn according to prescribed ritual formulas.

WORSHIP REQUIREMENTS: Covens meet either weekly or bi-weekly (at the full and

    new moon), always in the evening. Worship in some (but not all) groups

    occurs in the nude.

OTHER SPECIFIC RELIGIOUS REQUIREMENTS OTHER THAN WORSHIP: (See "Basic Teach-

    ings or Beliefs" and "Ethical Practices.")

DIETARY LAWS OR RESTRICTIONS: None.

SPECIAL RELIGIOUS HOLIDAYS: Eight Sabbats, or festivals, important for

    witches to gather and attune themselves to natural rhythms and forces as

    the seasons change, are followed: February Eve (January 31), Spring

    Equinox (March 21), Beltane or May Eve (April 30), Summer *Solstice* or

    Midsummer (June 22), Lammas (July 31), Autumn *Equinox* (September 21),

    Samhain (October 31) and Yule or Winter *Solstice* (December 21).

FUNERAL AND BURIAL REQUIREMENTS: None. Recognition of the death of a coven

    member takes place in the coven, apart from the "body" of the deceased.

    Ritual tools or materials found among the remains of the deceased should

    be immediately returned to the family or members of the coven.

AUTOPSY: No restrictions.

CREMATIONS: No restrictions.

Position on Service, Basic Beliefs

UNIFORM APPEARANCE REQUIREMENTS: None.

POSITION ON SERVICE IN THE ARMED FORCES: None. Members include the full range from career military personnel to conscientious objectors.

IS A PRIESTESS OR PRIEST REQUIRED AT TIME OF DEATH? No, but it would be permissable for any Chaplain to offer spiritual comfort at such times. Upon death, a prayer may be directed to God for the release of the soul from the Earth plane, separate and apart from any ritual work done by the member's coven.

ANY OTHER PRACTICES OR TEACHINGS WHICH MAY CONFLICT WITH MILITARY DIRECTIVES OR PRACTICES: None.

BASIC TEACHINGS OR BELIEFS: Gardnerians worship the Mother Goddess and also the Horned God, symbols of the basic polarity of all nature. They seek the balance within nature, within themselves, and between male and female. Worship is done in pairs, masculine and feminine, and the power which is produced by magical ritual is directed by the High Priestess for its desired purpose. While devotion to the Wiccan deities is the main coven activity, magick, the control and use of natural cosmic forces which emanate from the human body, is the secondary activity of the coven. It is done for healing, aiding members in various endeavors, and casting spells for people who request them. Witches believe in reincarnation, i.e., that the soul or spirit of the individual will progress through a number of subsequent Earthly lives as it evolves. Retribution for acts in this life will be returned threefold, good or evil, in this life. A reincarnated spirit starts afresh.

Literature, Ethics

CREEDAL STATEMENTS AND/OR AUTHORITATIVE LITERATURE: One book used by

Gardinerian Wicca as authoritative: The Book of Shadows, or book of

ritual. In the Gardnerian tradition, these are hand copied from High

Priestess to High Priestess. Each High Priestess then shares the infor-

mation with her coven. They are part of the traditional teachings of the

Craft, and are available only to initiates. From coven to coven, the

rituals vary slightly. The Gardnerian tradition is an evolved and evolv-

ing tradition. Hence, each coven will start with the materials passed on

to its High Priestess, and then experiment with new emphases, magical

formulas and rituals.

For an accurate historical picture of the Gardinerian Wicca, the

books of Gerald Gardner (Witchcraft Today and The Meaning of Witchcraft)

and Raymond Buckland (Witchcraft From The Inside and Witchcraft Ancient

and Modern) may be consulted.

ETHICAL PRACTICES: Gardnerian Witches live by the Wiccan Rede: "An Ye Harm

None, Do As Ye Will." Within this general concept is the Law of Retribu-

tion, by which witches can expect to receive threefold return on their

actions.

Social forces generally do not yet allow witches to publicly

declare their religious faith without fear of reprisals such as loss of

job, ridicule, etc. Rituals, many teachings, and even acknowledgement of

affiliation with the Craft are generally not discussed with non-initiates.

Ritual instruments are generally hidden and protected.

GARDNERIAN WICCA	Page 6

Recruiting, Relationships

HOW DOES GARDNERIAN WICCA RECRUIT MEMBERS? Wicca does not *proselytize* or

advertise for members. Growth comes through word of mouth. Inquirers are

screened, which might include participation in a public *Pagan* Grove,

where rituals are practiced, oriented on natural rhythms and the

Pagan dieties.

RELATIONSHIP WITH OTHER RELIGIONS: Wicca is open toward other faiths, recog-

nizing that the Great Mother appears in these faiths under various names.

Because of the persecutions of past years, Wiccans take a guarded

relation to groups which claim to possess "the Truth" or to be the

"Only Way." Wicca is only one path among many, and is not for everyone.

Members are encouraged to learn about all faiths, and are permitted to

attend services of other faiths, should they desire to do so.

NATIVE AMERICAN CHURCH
c/o Lawrence Gilpin, President
Macy, Nebraska 68039

Lawrence Gilpin

HISTORICAL ROOTS: The use of various drugs that alter the consciousness of the worshiper has a long history in world religion. In Pre-Columbian America, the peyote cactus, which contains mescaline, a consciousness-altering substance, was used by the Aztecs and their descendants. By the nineteenth century the practice was firmly entrenched in the Indian tribes of Mexico and in the years following the American Civil War spread to the tribes of the southwest -- the Mescalero Apache (1870), the Kiowa, and the Comanche. From these it spread to the tribes of the Plains and into Oklahoma, where its use aided the "vision search" so integral to Plains' religious quest.

In the 1890s the use of peyote was taken up by Prophet John Wilson in the Ghost Dance Movement, a prophetic movement that preached a return to the old ways in the face of white encroachments and reservation life. When the Ghost Dance died away, peyote remained and continued to spread. As its use grew, two trends emerged. One set of peyote users had a traditional orientation, while a second group were Christian. Both groups function within the Native American Church, and their existence account for the wide variety of practices encountered.

CURRENT WORLD LEADER: The Church is headed by a national president, elected for a two-year term. Present President is Lawrence Gilpin, a member of the Omaha Tribe.

ORIGINS IN THE U.S.: The formalization of a "church" among peyote users came in direct response to growing opposition from the government, the Indian missionaries and even fellow-tribe members. As early as 1896, the Oto

NATIVE AMERICAN CHURCH	Page 2
Origins, Organization, Leadership	

ORIGINS (continued): Church of the First Born was incorporated, the first of
several like bodies among various tribes. Then in 1918 an intertribal
group led in the formation of the Native American Church in response to
a proposal by the Bureau of Indian Affairs to have Congress pass an
anti-peyote law. By 1944 the Church had spread across the United
States and became the "Native American Church of the United States."
Continual spread led eleven years later to its becoming the "Native
American Church of North America."

NUMBER OF ADHERENTS IN THE U.S.: Approximately 225,000.

ORGANIZATIONAL STRUCTURE: The Native American Church is organized at three
levels. On the national level, an annual convention speaks for the
Church and elects officers. The President and other officers serve
two-year terms.

Representation to the national convention is by chapters, which may
consist of all Church members of the Church of one tribe in a single
area (usually a state). Each chapter has two votes at the national
convention. The chapter is further divided into congregations (one or
more). Each congregation is organized democratically and is the focus
of worship.

LEADERSHIP AND ROLE OF PRESIDENTS: The organization of local congregations
is under the leadership of democratically elected Presidents. Presidents
are responsible for all Church activities with the possible exception of
the worship service itself.

NATIVE AMERICAN CHURCH   Page 3

Worship, Requirements

WHO MAY CONDUCT WORSHIP SERVICES? In some traditions a priest leads the

    worship and is assisted by the firechief (who keeps the fire going) and

    the drummer. In others, the elder men lead.

IS GROUP WORSHIP REQUIRED? No, but it is integral to the regular practice

    of the faith.

WORSHIP REQUIREMENTS: Services will be held weekly, bi-weekly, or monthly

    in different congregations. They begin in the evening and last until

    dawn. Besides the ingestion of peyote, the service includes as a

    closing act a ceremonial meal in which water, corn, fruit, and dried

    beef are shared.

MINIMUM EQUIPMENT FOR WORSHIP: Peyote, fire (often in the form of live

    coals), water drum, gourd rattle, and staff. Individual congregations

    may require additional items.

FACILITIES FOR WORSHIP: Facilities vary. Some groups meet in homes, but

    many groups meet in a designated hogan or teepee. The worship space

    contains an altar and fireplace. The traditional hogans will have a

    moon-shaped altar, the Christian ones a cross-shaped altar with a

    Bible on it.

OTHER SPECIFIC RELIGIOUS REQUIREMENTS OTHER THAN WORSHIP: None.

DIETARY LAWS OR RESTRICTIONS: None.

SPECIAL RELIGIOUS HOLIDAYS: Most congregations will celebrate Thanksgiving,

    Easter, Christmas, New Year's, and Armistice Day. There are special

    services on the birthdays of individuals, days of mourning and for

    healing.

NATIVE AMERICAN CHURCH   Page 4

Requirements, Position on Service, Basic Beliefs

FUNERAL AND BURIAL REQUIREMENTS: Protestant services are acceptable for

   members.

AUTOPSY: No restrictions.

CREMATION: Not allowed.

MEDICAL TREATMENT: No restrictions; however, the peyote ceremony is used for

   healing the body.

UNIFORM APPEARANCE REQUIREMENTS: None.

POSITION ON SERVICE IN THE ARMED FORCES: None.

IS A PRIEST OR CLERGYPERSON REQUIRED AT TIME OF DEATH? No.

ANY OTHER PRACTICES OR TEACHINGS WHICH MAY CONFLICT WITH MILITARY DIRECTIVES

   OR PRACTICE: None, other than the use of peyote itself.

BASIC TEACHINGS OR BELIEFS: The Christian members of the Native American

   Church acknowledge a Triune God -- Father, Son and Holy Spirit. The

   Traditional members speak only of God. All believe in brotherly

   love, often expressed as three principles of respect for all people,

   compassion for all people and forgiveness for all people.

      Peyote is considered a sacrament and is venerated. It is eaten as

   a means of communing with the Spirit of the Almighty. Members refer to

   Romans 14:6 as a Biblical reference related to the taking of peyote:

   "He who eats anything does it to the honor of the Lord, for he gives

   thanks to God for the food."

      The Native American Church is the only religious body who have

   received court permission to use in their religious practices what

   is otherwise an illegal substance.

NATIVE AMERICAN CHURCH	Page 5

Practices Literature, Ethics, Recruiting

CREEDAL STATEMENTS AND/OR AUTHORITATIVE LITERATURE: None, though the
Christian congregations use the Bible extensively. For information on
the Native American Church, consult The Peyote Story by Bernard Roseman;
The Peyote Cult by Weston La Barre and The Peyote Religion by J.S.
Slotkin.

ETHICAL PRACTICES: In general, the Native American Church teaches its members
to live a high ethical life and is against immoral conduct. Alcohol and
dangerous drugs are forbidden. They also teach respect and humility in
the presence of one's elders.

HOW DOES THE NATIVE AMERICAN CHURCH RECRUIT MEMBERS? The Church spreads by
word-of-mouth and among people who have read of it in books and periodicals. It does not *proselyte*. Members are drawn from the American
Indian, more properly known as the Native American, community.

UNIVERSAL LIFE CHURCH	Bishop Kirby J. Hensley, D.D.
601 Third Street	President
Modesto, California 95351	

HISTORICAL ROOTS: The Universal Life Church was born out of the vision of
its founder Kirby S. Hensley. Hensley, born in 1911, was a self-educated
Baptist minister who became deeply influenced by his reading in world
religion. He began to conceive of a church that would on the one hand
offer a complete freedom of religion, and could, on the other hand,
bring all people of all religions together, instead of separating
them. Out of his growing conviction, Hensley founded the Universal
Life Church in 1962.

CURRENT WORLD LEADER: Bishop Kirby J. Hensley, Founder and President.

ORIGIN IN THE U.S.: (See "Historical Roots")

NUMBER OF MEMBERS IN THE U.S.: As of March, 1977, over 6,000,000 ministers
had been ordained and 25,000 had formed congregations which held regular meetings. Many of these are small congregations working on a
"house church" model.

ORGANIZATIONAL STRUCTURE: The Universal Life Church has a very loose structure. Rev. Hensley ordains anyone who wishes by presenting them with
a certificate and a set of instructions on how to form a congregation.
Each member-minister relates directly to the Rev. Hensley and the
National Office. Congregations are completely autonomous. The Church
operates the Universal Life University located in Modesto. The university offers courses by mail as well as classes for resident students.

LEADERSHIP AND ROLE OF MINISTERS: Ministers ordained by the Universal Life
Church may perform any functions normally associated with the clergy,

UNIVERSAL LIFE CHURCH	Page 2

Leadership, Worship, Requirements

LEADERSHIP AND ROLE OF MINISTERS (continued): including conducting of weddings, funerals, etc. Specific roles are determined by the minister and the local congregation.

WHO MAY CONDUCT WORSHIP SERVICES? Anyone.

IS GROUP WORSHIP REQUIRED? No. But local congregations are required to hold regular meetings.

WORSHIP REQUIREMENTS: None.

MINIMUM EQUIPMENT FOR WORSHIP: None.

FACILITIES FOR WORSHIP: Varies from congregation to congregation.

OTHER SPECIFIC RELIGIOUS REQUIREMENTS FOR WORSHIP: The Universal Life Church allows its congregations complete freedom of worship. While it makes no specific worship requirements, individual congregations may, and such requirements are respected.

DIETARY LAWS OR RESTRICTIONS: None.

SPECIAL RELIGIOUS HOLIDAYS: The Universal Life Church has no specific holidays, though local congregations celebrate a wide variety of them. There are two gatherings (conventions) each year in the spring and in the fall, at which the members and ministers meet for celebration and to conduct business.

FUNERAL AND BURIAL REQUIREMENTS: None.

AUTOPSY: No restrictions.

CREMATION: No restrictions.

MEDICAL TREATMENTS: No restrictions.

UNIVERSAL LIFE CHURCH   Page 3

Position on Service, Basic Beliefs, Recruiting, Relationships

UNIFORM APPEARANCE REQUIREMENTS: None.

POSITION ON SERVICE IN THE ARMED FORCES: Respect individual opinion, but the
   Universal Life Church is currently applying for chaplaincy positions for
   several of its ministers.

IS A PRIEST OR CLERGY PERSON REQUIRED AT TIME OF DEATH? No.

ANY OTHER PRACTICES OR TEACHINGS WHICH MIGHT CONFLICT WITH MILITARY DIRECTIVES
   OR PRACTICES: None.

BASIC TEACHINGS OR BELIEFS: The Universal Life Church has only one belief.
   They believe in that which is right and in every person's right to
   interpret what is right.

CREEDAL STATEMENTS AND/OR AUTHORITATIVE LITERATURE: The Universal Life
   Church has no creed or authoritative book such as the Bible. Those
   wishing to learn about the Church can obtain its periodical Universal
   Life and other materials that it publishes from the national office.

ETHICAL GUIDELINES: No specific guidelines except to do "what is right."

HOW DOES THE UNIVERSAL LIFE CHURCH RECRUIT MEMBERS? Recruitment has been
   primarily by word-of-mouth of the members. The Church has received
   widespread publicity that has brought many inquiries, and a few local
   congregations have advertised.

RELATIONSHIPS WITH OTHER RELIGIONS: The Universal Life Church is open
   and accepting of people of all religions. It is opposed only to
   those religions that attempt to deny religious freedom.

APPENDIX

APPROVING AUTHORITIES AND CONSULTANTS

The following individuals, associated with the groups addressed in this Handbook, were consulted regarding the accuracy of the individual descriptions for their group. Where these individuals have reviewed and approved the final draft description as developed, their name is preceded by the designation (A). Where an individual was consulted during the development of the description but did not actually see and approve the final version, their name is preceded by the designation (C). If no address is given in the list below, the cited authority can receive mail through the indicated address of group headquarters If the address for the authority is different from that given from the group, the address appears immediately below their name, if it is available.

The list is organized in the sequence of the groups as they appear in the Handbook.

CHRISTIAN HERITAGE GROUPS

Berkeley Christian Coalition	(A) Woodrow Nichols, Staff Member
Children of God	(A) Matt Child, Information Officer
Church of Christ, Scientist	(A) J. Buroughs Stokes, Manager Committees on Publication
Church of Jesus Christ of Latter Day Saints	(A) Elder Marion D. Hanks Counselor to the President
General Conference of Seventh-Day Adventists	(A) Elder Clark Smith, Director National Service Organization
Holy Order of MANS	(A) Rt. Rev. Andrew Rossi, Steward Esoteric Council
Holy Spirit Association for the Unification of World Christianity	(A) Susan Reinbold, Director of Public Affairs

CHRISTIAN HERITAGE GROUPS (continued)

International Christian Ministries   (A) Duane Pederson, Chaplain

Mennonite Church   (A) Ivan J. Kauffman, General Secretary

Religious Society of Friends in the U.S.   (A) Lorton G. Heusel, General Secretary Friends United Meeting

Reorganized Church of Jesus Christ of Latter Day Saints   (A) Colonel Pershing Tousley, Chairman Committee on Ministry to Armed Forces Personnel

Watchtower Bible and Tract Society of New York, Inc.   (A) W.L. Barry, Vice President

Worldwide Church of God   (A) Herman L. Hoeh, Minister

INDIAN HERITAGE GROUPS

Divine Light Mission   (A) Joe Anctil, Public Information Department

International Society for Krishna Consciousness   (A) Rupanuga das Adhikari, Regional Secretary

World Plan Executive Council   (A) Norin Isquith, National Staff

ISLAMIC GROUPS

Hanafi Muslims   (C) Imam Inrahim
Mosque Umar
137 E. 115th
Chicago, Illinois 60628

The Sufi Order   (A) Sikander Copplman, Staff

World Community of Islam in the West   (C) Minister Donnel Kareem, Assistant to the Chief Imam

JAPANESE HERITAGE GROUPS

Buddhist Churches of America   (A) Rev. Kenryu T. Tsuji, Presiding Bishop

JAPANESE HERITAGE GROUPS (continued)

Church of Perfect Liberty   (A) Rev. Kingo Inamura (Oya)
Director
North American Mission

Nichiren Shoshu Academy   (A) Guy C. McCloskey
Executive Secretary

JEWISH GROUPS

Black Hebrew Israelite Nation   (C) Anonymous Member

Conservative Jews   (A) Rabbi Stanley Rabinowitz
Rabbinical Assembly

Orthodox Jews   (A) Rabbi Israel Klaven
Rabbinical Council of
America

Reconstructionist Jews   (A) Rabbi Ludwig Nadelmann
Jewish Reconstructionist
Foundation

Reform Jews   (A) Rabbi Malcolm H. Stern
Director of Rabbinic Placement

SIKH GROUPS

Healthy, Happy, Holy Organization   (A) Sahib Sat-Peter Singh
Khalsa (see below)

Sikh Dharma   (A) Singh Sahib Sat-Peter Singh
Khalsa
Director, Community Relations
1521 Connecticut Avenue, N.W.
Washington, D.C.   20036

OTHER GROUPS

American Council of Witches   (A) Carl L. Weschcke, Publisher
Llewellyn Publications
(High Priest, St. Paul)

Baha'i Faith   (A) Ouida Coley
National Information Office

OTHER GROUPS (continued)

Church of Satan	(A)	John M. Kincaid Minister of Information
Church of Scientology	(A)	Greg L. Taylor Ministry of Public Affairs (DC)
Foundation Faith of the Millenium	(A)	Father Raphael, Luminary
Gardinerian Wicca	(A)	Lady Theos, High Priestess
Native American Church	(C)	Benjamin Bear Skin, President Illinois Chapter (Address uncertain)
Universal Life Church	(A)	Bishop Kirby J. Hensley President

GLOSSARY OF TERMS

AGENCY - Related to the concept of human freedom; the element of human life
that embodies the capacity to make decisions and choices that may have
both temporal and eternal implications.

ANTHROPOMORPHIC - Described or thought of as having human form or attributes

CANON - The body of scripture which is considered by a church to be official
and authoritative for its membership.

CHALICE - Sacred drinking cup used for the eucharist or for similar celebrations, depending on group and tradition.

DISFELLOWSHIPPED - To be removed for cause from the fellowship of a given
church or group.

ECCLESIASTICAL - Relating to a formal and established religious institution, normally associated with a group or body of clergy, or with a
church having specific structures and disciplines associated with
religious functions.

ECLECTIC - Selecting what appears to be best or most pertinent from various doctrines. Technically different than ecumenical, in that it is
related to specific doctrines, rather than to the commonality in all.

EFFICACIOUS - Literally, having the power to produce the desired effect.
Frequently used in terms of describing the total effectiveness of a
religious event; as in the "efficacious work of Jesus," meaning its
total effectiveness for salvation, reconciliation, etc.

EQUINOXES - Either of two times each year when the sun crosses the equator
and day and night throughout the world are of equal length (@ March 21
and September 23).

GLOSSARY OF TERMS (continued)

NOVITIATE - A person admitted to probationary membership, particularly in
terms of a probationary period for training for a religious community.

ORDINATION - To invest officially (in most groups, by the laying on of
hands) with ministerial or priestly authority. In most groups, this
will relate to one deemed to be "called" to minister.

PAGAN - Derived from the Latin "paganus," the term technically means "of
the country." In general, it relates to religions in which Nature is
seen as the immediate source of life, wisdom, health, or energy. Used
in terms of magickal and mystical experiences particularly.

PATEN - Plate, usually made of precious metal, used to carry the eucharis-
tic bread or other element of celebration, depending on group and
tradition.

PHYLACTERIES - Small leather boxes containing slips inscribed with scripture
passages. These traditionally are worn by Jewish men on the left arm
and forehead during morning weekday prayers.

PROGRESSIVE REVELATION - The belief that God reveals Himself progressively
over time, that human knowledge brings with its development the further
knowledge and understanding of the nature of God and His purpose for
humankind.

PROSELYTIZING - The inducing or recruiting of persons to become followers
of certain beliefs or practices. Frequently associated with strong
negative or positive influence exerted on members of other faiths.

GLOSSARY OF TERMS (continued)

SACRAMENTAL ORDINANCES - Rites and ceremonies believed to have been instituted or affirmed within a religious tradition by God or by the founder
of the religion. In Christianity, for example, these are those ceremonies instituted or affirmed by Christ.

SAKYAMUNI - A name of the Gautama Buddha.

SOLSTICES - One of the two points on the eliptic at which its distance
from the celestial equator is greatest and which is reached by the
Sun each year at approximately June 22 and December 22.

TITHING - The practice of contributing a tenth (10%) of one's salary or income toward the support or furthering of a religious activity. Generally viewed as voluntary.

ZION - The concept which points to the Christian mission to build God's
kingdom on earth.

INDEX OF TERMS

INDEX OF TERMS (continued)

INDEX OF TERMS (continued)

INDEX OF TERMS (continued)

INDEX OF TERMS (continued)

Talmud, V-11, 18, 24
Taoism, IV-2
Teachings of Yogi Bhajan, VI-5
Teens for Christ, I-3, 11
Tenrikyo or Tenri Kyo, IV-2

Thetan, VII-27
Theos, Lady, VII-36
Theosophical Society, VII-1
Three HO (3HO) Foundation, VI-2, 3f.
TM, II-3, 17f.
Traditional Witchcraft, VII-3, 5f.

Transcendental Meditation, II-3, 17f.
Tripitaka, IV-3, 9

UAHC, V-25f.
"unclean" foods, I-31, 77 (see also
    V-15)
Unification Church, I-3, 41f.
Unification Theological Seminary, I-42
Union of American Hebrew Congregations
    (UAHC), V-25f.
Union of Orthodox Jewish Congregations,
    V-13f.
United Church of Religious Science, I-3
United Synagogue of America, V-7f.
Unity School of Christianity, I-3

Universal House of Justice, VII-11,
    15f.
Universal Life, VII-49
Universal Life University, VII-47
Upanishads, II-1

Vaishnava, II-2, 11f.
Veda, Vedic scriptures, II-1, 11
Vedanta, II-2f.
Vedanta Society, II-2, III-9
Vishnu, II-3, VI-1
Voices of Freedom, I-42
Voodoo, VII-17

Walpurgisnacht, VII-17, 19
Watchtower, The, I-73
White, Ellen G., I-29, 32.
Wicca, VII-3, 5f., 35f.
Williams, George, IV-17

Witchcraft, Witches, VII-2f., 5f., 35f.
World Tribune, IV-20

Yeshiva University, V-14
Yoga, various disciplines of, II-1f.
Yoga, Kundalini, VI-3f. (see also II-2)
Yogi Bhajan, VI-2, 3f., 7f.
Young, Brigham, I-2, 23

Young Buddist Association, IV-6

Zen, Zen Buddhism, IV-2
Zoroastrian magi, III-9

Printed in the United States
27851LVS00001B/11

9 780898 756074